THEMATIC
Multicultural
FOLK TALES

Written by David Jefferies

Illustrated by Sue Fullam and Keith Vasconcelles

Teacher Created Materials, Inc.
P.O. Box 1040
Huntington Beach, CA 92647
©1992 Teacher Created Materials, Inc.
Made in U.S.A.

ISBN 1-55734-230-X

WESTERN EDUCATIONAL ACTIVITIES LTD.
12006 - 111 Ave. Edmonton, Alberta T5G 0E6
Ph: (403) 413-7055   Fax: (403) 413-7056

Table of Contents

Introduction

Multicultural Folk Tales uses stories from the African and Eskimo traditions to help students understand how folk tales from all over the world share similar characteristics. In its 80 pages of thematically-unified, integrated activities, students will experience the stories and learn about the cultures which created them. The centerpieces of the unit are *Mufaro's Beautiful Daughters*, an African folk tale, and *Song of Sedna,* an Eskimo folk tale. Included in this unit are creative, introductory activities to draw students into the world of each story, writing and critical thinking activities, and projects to help students apply their knowledge to the world around them. A culminating project and activities in language arts, math, science, social studies, performing arts, and cooking help extend story concepts into every part of the curriculum. This very complete resource will be a welcome time saver for busy teachers.

This thematic unit includes:

❏ **literature selections**—summaries of two children's books with related activities

❏ **planning guides**—daily suggestions for sequencing lessons

❏ **writing ideas**—daily suggestions, including Big Books

❏ **homework suggestions**—extending the unit into the home

❏ **curriculum connections**—in language arts, math, science, social studies, art, and life skills

❏ **group projects**—to foster cooperative learning

❏ **culminating activity**—to help students apply their knowledge in the world around them

❏ **bibliography**—suggestions for additional books on the theme

> **To keep this valuable resource intact year after year, punch holes in the pages and store them in a three-ring binder.**

Introduction *(cont.)*

Why Whole Language?

A whole language approach involves children using all modes of communication: reading, writing, listening, observing, illustrating, and speaking. Communication skills are integrated into lessons which emphasize the whole of language rather than isolating its parts. A child reads, writes, speaks, listens, and thinks in response to a literature experience introduced by the teacher. In this way, language skills grow naturally, stimulated by involvement and interest in the topic at hand.

Why Thematic Planning?

One useful tool for implementing an integrated whole language program is thematic planning. By choosing a theme with corresponding literature selections for a unit of study, a teacher can plan activities throughout the day that lead to a cohesive, in-depth study of the topic. Students practice and apply their skills in meaningful contexts. Consequently, they tend to learn and retain more. Both teachers and students are freed from a day that is broken into unrelated segments of isolated drill and practice.

Why Cooperative Learning?

In addition to academic skills and content, students need to learn social skills. No longer can this area of development be taken for granted. Students must learn to work cooperatively in groups in order to function well in modern society. Group activities should be a regular part of school life, and teachers should consciously include social objectives as well as academic objectives in their planning. The teacher should clarify and monitor the qualities of good group interaction just as he/she would clarify and monitor the academic goals of a project.

Why Big Books?

An excellent cooperative, whole language activity is the production of Big Books. Groups of students or the entire class can apply their language skills and content knowledge to create additions to the classroom library. These books make excellent culminating projects for sharing beyond the classroom with parents and friends. This thematic unit includes directions for making Big Books in your classroom.

Mufaro's Beautiful Daughters

By John Steptoe

Summary

Two daughters, Manyara and Nyasha, live with their father in a small African village. Manyara is selfish and vain, but Nyasha is unselfish and kind. One day a messenger comes and announces that the king is looking for a wife. Mufaro asks both of his daughters to go to the city where the king lives. As they journey to the city, both daughters meet challenges along the way. Children will respond to the classic plot of the story and will be interested in how justice prevails in the end.

The outline below is a suggested plan for using the various activities in this unit. You may need to adapt this plan to meet the needs of your particular class.

Sample Plan

Lesson I

- Do What Is a Folk Tale? (page 70) using several favorite folk tales
- Daily Writing Topics (page 39)
- Features of the African Continent (page 10)
- Bantu Language Family (page 7)

Lesson II

- Continue Daily Writing Topics
- Read *Mufaro's Beautiful Daughters*
- Use Mapping the Story (page 15)
- Countries of Africa (page 55)
- Graphing the Languages (page 45)

Lesson III

- Continue Daily Writing Topics
- Reread *Mufaro's Beautiful Daughters*

- Guess the Character (page 13)
- The Ruins of Zimbabwe (page 12)
- How Green is Your Snake? (page 59)
- Mapping the Continent (page 58)

Lesson IV

- Continue Daily Writing Topics
- Do Nyasha's Problem (page 46)
- Reread *Mufaro's Beautiful Daughters*
- Quartering the Story (page 42)
- Read *Makanda Mahlanu* (pages 21-24)
- Comparing the Stories (page 19)
- Try an African Recipe (page 66)

Lesson V

- Continue Daily Writing Topics
- Scrambled Summary (page 17)
- Galimoto (page 59)
- African Games (page 61)

Overview of Activities

Setting the Stage

1. Introduce the topic of folk tales by having children recall several favorites: for example, *Cinderella, The Frog Prince, Jack and the Beanstalk.* Brainstorm what makes these stories alike. Use page 70 to analyze the favorite tales identified by students. Tell students that you will begin your folk tale unit with a story from Africa.

2. Draw an outline of Africa on the board and ask the students to guess what it is. Ask them what they think of when they hear the word "Africa." Cluster responses on the board, and use them later as a resource for vocabulary exercises.

Overview of Activities *(cont.)*

3. Do Features of the African Continent (page 10). Use the Africa outline you drew on the board to model where to put some of Africa's geographic features.

4. Introduce the Daily Writing Topics (page 39). Continue these each day.

5. Introduce the Bantu Language Family (page 7). Have students practice the vocabulary cards in pairs or in groups. Integrate these words into the unit when possible. Challenge students to make their own picture flashcards for these words: *kukondwa* (happiness), *bwana buzydale* (freedom), *umuzya* (silence), and *yanda* (love).

Enjoying the Book

1. Read the first paragraph of the book. Explain that people sometimes take a story and tell it in their own version. Ask why John Steptoe, an Afro-American author, might feel a special connection to the folk tales of Africa. Why would he dedicate his book to the children of South Africa?

2. Read the story to the class. Afterward discuss the main ideas. Talk about the differences between Nyasha and Manyara, why the king changes shapes, and the king's tests as being central to the story's meaning. Discuss how this story is similar to other folk tales.

3. Reread the story using Mapping the Story (page 15).

4. Teach students about six African countries with Countries of Africa (page 55).

5. Increase students' knowledge of languages by doing Graphing the Languages (page 45).

6. Read the book 3 or 4 times. Focus on a different aspect of the story (setting, characters, animals, etc.) with each reading. Do Guess the Character (page 13).

7. Divide the class into groups. Have them do The Ruins of Zimbabwe (page 12). This will give students an understanding of African history. Have books available about Zimbabwe if possible.

8. Do How Green is Your Snake? (page 59).

9. Do Mapping the Continent (page 58) and discuss why mapmakers use different colors to distinguish the borders of countries. Ask students which continent has the most countries. (Africa)

10. Have students do Nyasha's Problem (page 46).

11. Reread *Mufaro's Beautiful Daughters* and give students Quartering the Story (page 42).

12. Explain that this story is told in many places in Africa, and names and events are often changed in other versions. Read *Makanda Mahlanu* (pages 21-24). Have students do Comparing the Stories (page 19) to learn the differences and similarities between the two stories.

Extending the Book

1. Do Galimoto (page 59). Challenge students to make their own toys with everyday materials.

2. Use Scrambled Summary (page 17) and make a Big Book version of *Mufaro's Beautiful Daughters*.

3. Have students write and illustrate their own folk tales by making changes in the story.

4. Make some African Recipes (page 66). Play African games (page 61).

Bantu Language Family

A language family is a group of languages which develop and change slowly and are related to a single language, called a parent language. When speakers of the parent language move apart and lose contact with each other, their language begins to change. As time passes, several new languages develop.

Makanda Mahlanu is an African folk tale written in Bantu language. Bantu is a name for a family of languages spoken throughout southern Africa. Some speakers of different languages in the Bantu family can still talk to each other because the languages are similar. Other languages in the Bantu family are so different that two people cannot understand each other at all.

Below are twelve words in a Bantu language called Botatwe. Read the sentences and look at the pictures on pages 8 and 9 to find the meaning of each word. Write the meaning in the blank. Your teacher will give you pages 8 and 9 to make flashcards so you can practice your new words.

1. A *tata* is someone who might carry a child on his shoulders. Who is a *tata*? _____

2. You might find an *iduba* in a vase. What is an *iduba*? _____

3. You will definitely want to avoid a *syaanza*'s sharp teeth.
   What is a *syaanza*? _____

4. A *sokwe* swings from tree to tree. What is a *sokwe*? _____

5. "*Wa buka*," my brother said as he came down to breakfast.
   What does *wa buka* mean? _____

6. Beat a great rhythm on the *ingoma*. What does *ingoma* mean? _____

7. A *mwana* is playing on the swing. What does *mwana* mean? _____

8. A *musa* is someone you can count on. What does *musa* mean? _____

9. You gave me fruit. I say, "*Nda lumba*." What does *nda lumba* mean? _____

10. My *bamama* cooks me dinner after she comes home from work.
    What does *bamama* mean? _____

11. At night the reflection of the *mwezi* shines on the water.
    What does *mwezi* mean? _____

12. A huge *inzovu* crashes through the brush. What does *inzovu* mean? _____

On the back of this page, write your own sentences using each Bantu vocabulary word.

Bantu Flashcards

Use page 7 to write the correct Bantu word on each line.

Bantu Flashcards *(cont.)*

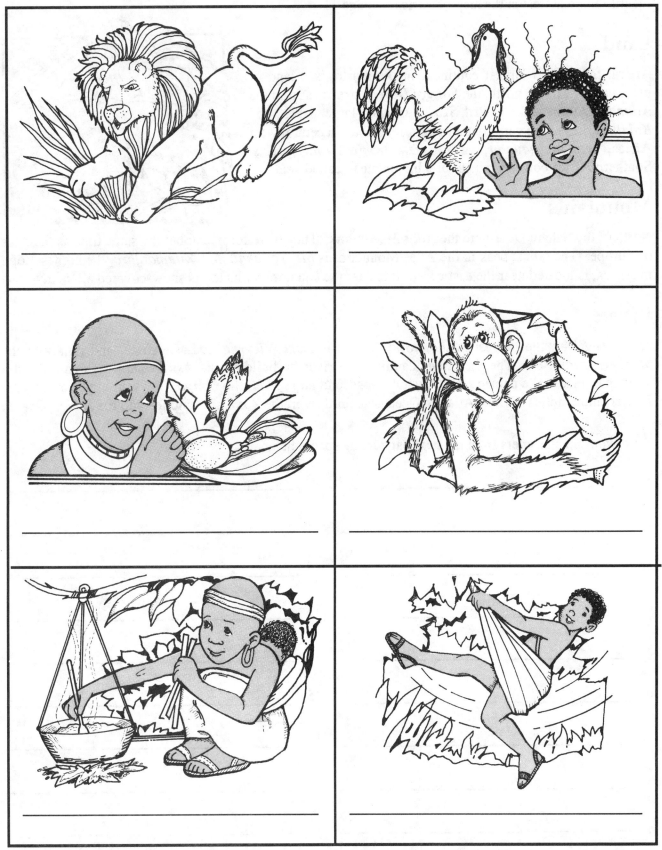

Features of the African Continent

Read the following paragraphs about Africa. Use the bold, italicized clues and an encyclopedia to identify the features on the map of Africa on page 11.

Land

Africa, the second largest continent in the world, is a land of great variety. In the north, the *Sahara Desert* stretches from the *Atlantic Ocean* to the *Red Sea.* Another large desert, the *Kalahari*, lies in the very southern part of Africa. In central west Africa, near the *equator*, grow great *tropical rain forests*. Southern Africa consists mostly of a high plateau called *veld*.

Mountains

North of the Sahara Desert are the *Atlas Mountains*. They were formed about the same time as the Alps of Europe. The tallest peak in the Atlas Mountains is *Mt. Toubkai*. *Mt. Kilamanjaro*, the highest point in Africa, is located near the east coast. It is near the equator, yet its top is snow-covered all year.

Rivers

The *Nile River*, the longest in the world, begins in *Lake Victoria* in East Africa, and runs into the *Mediterranean Sea*. The Egyptians dammed the river by building the *Aswan Dam* which created a large man-made lake named *Lake Nasser*. A second large river, the *Congo*, flows through tropical rain forests and empties into the Atlantic Ocean. A third river, the *Zambezi,* empties into the *Indian Ocean.*

Write your map answers from the next page in the spaces below.

1. _____
2. _____
3. _____
4. _____
5. _____
6. _____
7. _____
8. _____
9. _____

10. _____
11. _____
12. _____
13. _____
14. _____
15. _____
16. _____
17. _____
18. _____

10

Features of the African Continent
(cont.)

Use an encyclopedia and page 10 to help you identify each number. Write your answers on page 10.

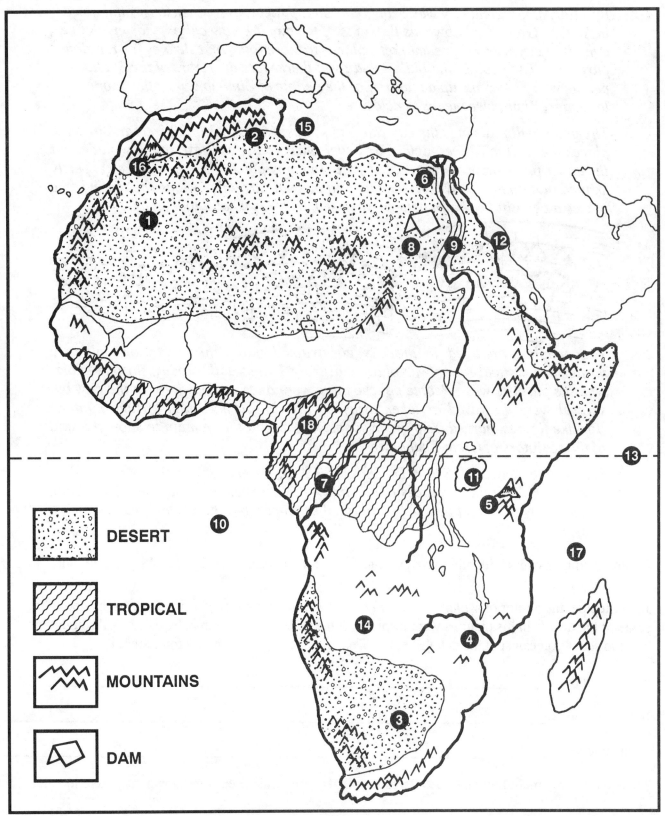

DESERT

TROPICAL

MOUNTAINS

DAM

The Ruins of Zimbabwe

Read the information below about the city of Zimbabwe with your group, and underline the main idea from each paragraph. Rewrite the main ideas in your own words.

By 1100 A.D. a great city was being built on a plateau in southeastern Zimbabwe in Africa. Great Zimbabwe, as the ruins of the city are now called, was much like a modern city with houses, markets, places to store food, and shrines for religious purposes. The people who built it and lived there were ancestors of the Shona people who now make up a majority of the people of Zimbabwe. In the Shona language, Zimbabwe means "enclosure."

The great wall that rings the city ranges in thickness from 3 to 20 feet, and in some places the wall is 20 feet high. The lower parts of the wall are roughly made, but the upper parts show a great deal of skill. In many places the stone was so expertly shaped that no mortar was needed to hold the wall together. Along the top in some places a beautiful chevron pattern was used. Here is what it looked like:

The people who lived in the city constructed many things. In one place a mysterious conical tower was built measuring 29 feet tall. Today, no one knows what its purpose was. People believe there were once many statues in the city, but several were destroyed or taken away by invading armies and fortune hunters. Birdlike figures, carved from green soapstone, are all that remain to show the skill of the sculptors of Great Zimbabwe.

Somewhere between 1500 A.D. and 1800 A.D. people deserted the city. Most scientists believe the resources of the area — like timber, salt, and the mines — had given out by then, and people moved to other places, but the actual reasons remain a mystery.

Compare your answers with other groups. Did they find the same main ideas? Why or why not?

John Steptoe, the author of *Mufaro's Beautiful Daughters*, explains on the first page of the book that some of the details in his pictures were inspired by the ruins of Great Zimbabwe. Look through the book to see if you can spot the details below. Describe the page where you found them.

Chevron pattern: _____

Soapstone birds: _____

Conical tower: _____

Make a drawing, including these details, to show how you think Great Zimbabwe may have looked.

Guess the Character

Help students increase their comprehension of the story by focusing on the traits and actions of specific characters.

Materials: copies of this page and page 14; envelopes; scissors

Directions

1. Ask students to help you list the characters in the story.

2. Have students form cooperative groups and write clues about each character on the cards below and on the next page. Model how to use descriptive sentences ("She is kind.") and action sentences ("He asks for food.").

3. After they have finished writing their clues, give each group an envelope for their cards. Have students cut on the dotted lines to make twelve cards, mixing up the clues and the pictures, and put them in the envelopes. Have groups exchange envelopes and read the clues and match them with the correct pictures.

4. For closure, discuss the different clues the class wrote. Which clues were most helpful? Which were confusing? Can some clues be used to describe more than one character?

Extension: Have students choose three classmates and write positive, descriptive clues about them for homework. Read the clues and have students guess about whom they were written.

Clue 1: _____

_____

Clue 2: _____

_____

Clue 3: _____

_____

King

Clue 1: _____

_____

Clue 2: _____

_____

Clue 3: _____

_____

Hungry Boy

Guess the Character (cont.)

Clue 1: _____

_____

Clue 2: _____

_____

Clue 3: _____

_____

Mufaro

Clue 1: _____

_____

Clue 2: _____

_____

Clue 3: _____

_____

Nyasha

Clue 1: _____

_____

Clue 2: _____

_____

Clue 3: _____

_____

Manyara

Clue 1: _____

_____

Clue 2: _____

_____

Clue 3: _____

_____

Old Woman

14

Mapping the Story

The purpose of this activity is to help students visualize the story setting. Read the story once to the class for enjoyment. Do this activity during a second reading.

Materials: copies of page 16; 18" x 24" (45 cm x 60 cm) sheets of construction paper; glue; scissors

Directions

1. Give one copy of page 16 to each student and have them cut out the cards.

2. Read the first page of the story aloud to your class. Ask them to describe what places are mentioned. Have students draw a river on their sheets of construction paper and glue down the cards of the African village and the city.

3. As you read the story to the class, have students glue down the cards for the garden, the forest, and palace. Tell students there are no exact answers. Have them follow the story by moving their character cards along their maps as you read. (Option: Do a large map in front of the class as the students make maps at their desks.)

4. After the story, have groups of students glue down characters on their maps representing different events of the story. Display the maps and have students guess which story event each map shows.

Mapping the Story (cont.)

Village	City	Palace
Forest	Garden	Nyasha
Manyara	Mufaro	Nyoka
Hungry Boy	Old Woman	King
Messenger	Laughing Trees	Man with Head

Scrambled Summary

Help! Someone has written a summary of *Mufaro's Beautiful Daughters*, but it's completely mixed up. Number the sentences below in the correct order. Cut out the sentences on the dashed lines and use them to make a Big Book. Ask your teacher for directions. (See page 18.)

_____ When they got to the city, they met a very scared Manyara.

_____ Manyara met a young boy who wanted food, but she was mean to him.

_____ Manyara was selfish, but Nyasha was kind.

_____ Instead of a monster, the king was the garden snake Nyasha had met in her own garden back in the village.

_____ Manyara became a servant in the queen's household.

_____ Mufaro decided to take both of his daughters, but Manyara snuck out at night to get there first.

_____ She had seen the king, and he had appeared as a monstrous, five-headed snake.

_____ A man named Mufaro had two beautiful daughters.

_____ But Nyasha went into the king's chamber anyway.

_____ The two were married, and everyone was invited to the great celebration.

_____ Nyasha gave the boy food and was kind to the old woman.

_____ Later she insulted an old woman and ignored a man with his head under his arm.

_____ The king sent a messenger to announce that the king was looking for a wife.

_____ The next day Mufaro and Nyasha set out on their journey.

Making Books

Materials: 18" x 24" (45cm x 60 cm) sheets of construction paper; lined writing paper; scissors; glue; hole punch; metal rings; colored pencils, crayons, or markers

Big Books

Directions

1. Have students in groups of two or three complete the Scrambled Summary, page 17.

2. Have students cut out their sentence strips and glue them to sheets of construction paper or rewrite sentences in their own words.

3. Have each group illustrate their sentences and make a book cover.

4. Have students put their pages in order.

5. Punch holes on the left side of each page and bind the big book together with metal rings.

6. Have students present their books aloud to another class.

7. Put the Big Books in the school library for other classes to read.

Pop-Up Books

Directions

1. Fold a piece of construction paper in half and cut two slits 1/2 way down the fold.

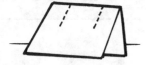

2. Push the cut area through the fold and crease it to form the pop-up section.

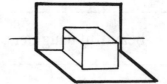

3. Make other pop-up pages and glue them back to back.

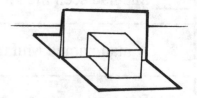

4. Write story sentences above the pop-up section and glue an appropriate picture from a magazine or a drawing to the pop-up page.

5. Glue a cover to the pop-up books.

Extension: Have groups of students write their own folk tale pop-up or Big Books by using the characteristics listed on What Is a Folk Tale?, page 70.

18

Comparing the Stories

Materials: copies of Venn diagram (page 20); *Makanda Mahlanu* (pages 21-24); copies of sentences below; glue; scissors; markers; butcher paper

Directions

1. Explain to students how stories change with time as people move from place to place and retell them. Describe how the story of *Mufaro's Beautiful Daughters* changed as people moved from village to village across Africa.

2. Read *Makanda Mahlanu* to your students. Challenge them to listen carefully for the differences and similarities between it and *Mufaro's Beautiful Daughters*.

3. Introduce the Venn diagram. Have students cut out and glue the sentences below in the correct spaces on the Venn diagram. Have students glue statements that are true about both stories in the center section.

4. Finish the lesson by drawing a large Venn diagram on butcher paper. Have students tell you where to write the sentences or have them fill in the diagram during independent work time. Afterward, review the answers with the class and resolve any differences of opinion.

Extension: Read another version of the folk tale called *The Talking Eggs* by Robert D. San Souci. Have students do a three-way Venn diagram with three intersecting circles using the three stories.

1. The two sisters are tested.
2. The good sister sees a five-headed snake.
3. There is a mouse in the story.
4. The king changes into many shapes.
5. The king appears as a five-headed snake.

6. The evil sister snuck away in the middle of the night to get ahead of the good sister.
7. The evil sister gets advice but doesn't listen to it.
8. How people look on the outside does not always show what they are like on the inside.
9. The good sister gives a little boy some food.

Venn Diagram

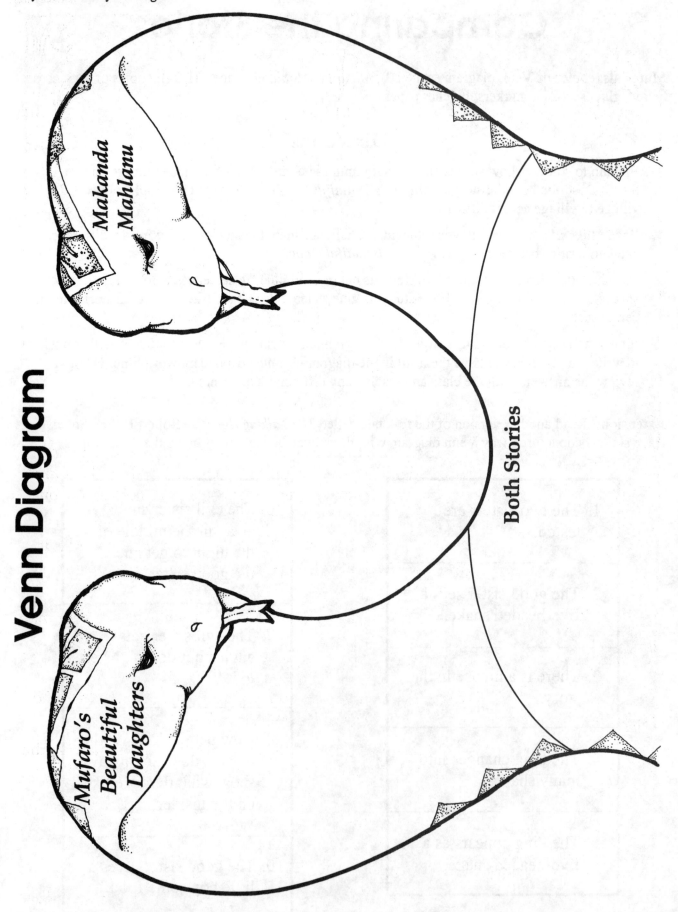

Makanda Mahlanu

Both Stories

Mufaro's Beautiful Daughters

Makanda Mahlanu

A Bantu Folk Tale from Africa

Retold by Josepha Sherman

Once, long ago, there lived a poor man with two daughters. Zikazi, the elder, was very beautiful. *Wau*, but she was also proud and lazy. Zanyana, the younger daughter, was beautiful, too, but unlike her sister, she was kind and sensible.

One day a messenger came to the poor man's little mud hut. "The great chief Makanda Mahlanu wishes to wed one of your daughters."

"But — but no one has ever seen the great chief!" the poor man protested. "No one even knows what he looks like."

"Wed one of us?" wondered Zanyana. "Which one?"

"Why me, of course!" cried haughty Zikazi. "I am older and more beautiful. The great chief shall wed me."

So off Zikazi went to the village of Makanda Mahlanu. On the way she met a mouse, which sat up on its hind legs and said in its tiny voice, "Shall I show you the way?"

" How dare a silly little mouse speak to me?" cried Zikazi. "Go away!"

The mouse ran away. Zikazi went on. But the path grew so narrow and so full of thorns that her leather dress was soon sadly torn and her face and arms all scratched. As she struggled on, she

Makanda Mahlanu *(cont.)*

met a frog. It croaked at her and said, "Shall I give you a warning?"

"How dare a slimy frog speak to me?" cried Zikazi. "Go away!"

The frog hopped off. But as it hopped, it called to Zikazi, "Foolish girl, I'll warn you anyway: When the trees laugh at you, don't laugh back at them!"

Zikazi thought that was nonsense. But just then the trees did start to laugh at her, shaking their branches in glee! "How dare you laugh at me?" cried Zikazi. "You—you silly twigs!" And she started to laugh back at them and mock them.

"Be wary, Zikazi," came a whispery voice, like the stirring of wind through leaves. "You did not listen to Mouse and Frog when they tried to help you. Foolish girl! You have but one chance left: Grind the millet well. Fear nothing you see."

"What foolishness," said Zikazi, and she went on her way.

When she came to the village of the great chief, with all its huts and herds of people, she went right up to the bridal hut. There the servants of Makanda Mahlanu gave her millet seeds to grind into a bridal cake. But Zikazi was such a lazy thing! She ground the seed only once, and the bridal cake was hard and lumpy as a rock.

Zikazi didn't care. "Let me see my husband," she said.

There came a slithering. There came a shivering. Suddenly Makanda Mahlanu was before her—and he was a monster! He was a huge snake with five staring heads! Zikazi forgot the warning of the trees. She ran away in fear, all the way back to her father's hut. There, scratched and shaking and dirty, she sobbed, "He's a monster! Makanda Mahlanu is a monster!"

But Zanyana thought to herself, I wonder. "Now it's my turn," she told her father, and though he tried to stop her, Zanyana set out for the village of the great chief. She hadn't gone far when the mouse sat up on its hind legs and asked her, "Shall I show you the way?"

"Yes, kind mouse, please do."

22

Makanda Mahlanu (cont.)

So the mouse led her to a broad, smooth path. Not a pebble bruised her feet, not a thorn tore her dress. She came to the frog, who called up, "Shall I give you a warning?"

"Yes, kind frog, please do."

So the frog warned her, "When the trees laugh at you, don't laugh back at them."

The trees laughed. Zanyana only smiled. "I guess a human being does look funny to you," she called up to them.

"Grind the millet well," said the whispery voice. "Fear nothing you see."

Zanyana nodded and went on. Soon she reached the village of the great chief. When she entered the bridal hut, the servants put the millet seeds before her for the bridal cake. Zanyana ground it once, she ground it twice, she ground it so well that the cake was smooth and fine and soft.

"Now," she asked softly, "may I see my husband-to-be?"

There came a slither, there came a shudder, and Makanda Mahlanu, the terrible five-headed snake, entered the hut. Zanyana gasped. But then she remembered what the trees had told her: "Fear nothing you see."

So she merely bowed politely before Makanda Mahlanu and said, "Husband-to-be, I am here."

"You do not fear me?"

The snake's voice was cool as water, but sad, so sad! Zanyana looked up and, *wau*, his eyes were so sad, too! But there was a hint of hope and a shining of such kindness in them that her heart sang with surprise. "Oh no," Zanyana said softly, "I don't fear you. I—I pity you."

"How can you pity me? I am so ugly!"

"Maybe the outer Makanda Mahlanu is a monster. But I think that the inner Makanda Mahlanu is not ugly at all."

The snake reared up its five terrible heads before her. "Could you like him?"

Makanda Mahlanu *(cont.)*

"Yes, I think I could."

"Could you love him?"

Love a monstrous snake? Zanyana fought not to shiver. But his eyes were still so very sad, as though he expected her to run away in terror, just like Zikazi. Why, how lonely he must be! How could she ever be cruel enough to run away from this poor unhappy being?

"Yes," Zanyana said firmly. "I could love him."

Makanda Mahlanu gave a great cry. His snake-form shook and shook till the walls of the hut cracked and nearly fell. Zanyana covered her eyes to protect them from the bits of flying mud and straw. But when she looked up again—the terrible five-headed snake was gone. It its place stood a tall, young man, so handsome and warm of eye that Zanyana's heart sang anew.

"I am Makanda Mahlanu," he said, and his voice was no longer sad. "Once I chased an evil wizard away from my people. In his anger, he cast a spell upon me: I should be a monstrous snake till the day someone should dare to love me. You've broken the spell, Zanyana! By your bravery and kindness, you have freed me." He laughed for joy. "You said you could love me when I wore a monster's shape. Can you love me now, my brave Zanyana? Will you be my wife?"

"I will," Zanyana said happily, "oh, I will, indeed!"

So it was. And they lived together in peace and joy.

First printed in *Cricket* magazine, February, 1990. Reprinted here by permission of Josepha Sherman.

24

Song of Sedna

By Robert D. San Souci

Summary

Many young men have come to marry the young Eskimo woman, Sedna, but she waits for the man she has seen in her dreams. When he arrives, Sedna goes with him in his umiak. He takes her to a strange new home where she finds that things are not always the way they appear. Students will enjoy following Sedna's journey as she encounters many dangers and grows in maturity to eventually become the goddess of the sea.

Sample Plan

Lesson I

- Daily Writing Topics (page 39)
- Peoples of the North (page 27)
- Eskimo games (page 63)
- Arctic and African Murals (page 51)
- Animal Number Clues (page 48)

Lesson II

- Continue Daily Writing Topics
- Fresh Water, Salt Water (page 49)
- Read *Song of Sedna*
- Introduce Readers' Theater (page 30) and Shadow Play (page 34)
- Story Ladder (page 29)

Lesson III

- Continue Daily Writing Topics
- Practice Shadow Play and Readers' Theater

- Do Counting in Aleut (page 47)
- Venn Diagram (page 75)
- Borrowed Words (page 44)

Lesson IV

- Continue Daily Writing Topics
- Reread *Song of Sedna*
- Make a Sociogram (page 40)
- Continue Arctic and African Murals
- Make Sugar Cube Igloos (page 60)
- Eskimos: Then and Now (page 38)
- Present Arctic and African Murals

Lesson V

- Continue Daily Writing Topics
- Make Pop-up or Big Books (page 18)
- Make an Amulet (page 60)
- Present Readers' Theater and Shadow Play
- Begin Culminating Activity (page 67-75)

Overview of Activities

Setting the Stage

1. Ask your students which group of people lives the farthest north in the coldest place on earth. Students will probably answer Eskimos. Explain that there are several different kinds of Eskimos, and that other groups of people also live in the northern regions. Introduce Peoples of the North (page 27). If possible, have some books on hand which show pictures of the Arctic regions.

2. Introduce Eskimo games (page 63). Explain that Eskimos use bone and string to make many of their games. Have students make games from materials in the classroom and at home. Give students time to experiment with the games. Discuss why these hand-eye coordination games are good for people who survive almost exclusively by hunting and fishing.

Overview of Activities *(cont.)*

3. Show the cover and selected scenic pictures from *Song of Sedna*. Discuss how the settings of *Mufaro's Beautiful Daughters* and *Song of Sedna* are different. What kinds of animals would students expect to live in each area? Use Arctic and African Mural (page 51) to continue the discussion. Schedule several 20-30 minute independent reading and research times for students to make animal murals.

4. Have students do Animal Number Clues (page 48) as homework to supplement Arctic and African Mural.

Enjoying the Book

1. Explain that the author is retelling a story Eskimos have told for hundreds of years. Review What is a Folk Tale? (page 70). Ask students to listen for the folk tale elements found in *Song of Sedna*.

2. Read the story to the class. Discuss how Sedna becomes goddess of the sea. Why would the goddess of the sea be important to the Eskimos? Describe how Eskimos depend on the sea for most of their food. Ask your students why Alaskan Eskimos are the only American citizens who are sometimes allowed to hunt whales. Do Fresh Water, Salt Water (page 49).

3. Introduce Readers' Theater (page 30) and Shadow Play (page 34). Have Readers' Theater actors practice while shadow puppet makers practice using their puppets. Present Readers' Theater together with the Shadow Play.

4. Have students do Story Ladder (page 29) and make Pop-up or Big Books (page 18).

5. Use a Venn diagram (page 75) to compare *Mufaro's Beautiful Daughters* with *Song of Sedna*.

6. Do Borrowed Words (page 44) to help students see the connection between African and Eskimo cultures and the English language.

7. Do a Sociogram of the story (page 40). Discuss how the relationships between characters are an important part of any story. Challenge students to make sociograms from their own stories they have written.

8. Make Sugar Cube Igloos (page 60).

Extending the Book

1. Do Eskimos Then and Now (page 38) to help students see the changes in Eskimo culture in the last 50 years as compared to Eskimo life in *Song of Sedna*.

2. Challenge students to make changes in the story and use Pop-Up Books as a way of depicting these changes to the class. Share and discuss story changes with the class.

3. Briefly discuss Mattak's amulet. Share and discuss why people use objects for luck. What are some other examples of good luck objects? Do Making an Amulet (page 60).

4. Read folk tales from other cultures. Explain that all cultures have folk tales, both oral and written. Do the Culminating Activity on pages 67-75 to give students an opportunity to learn more about the richness, unity, and diversity of human storytelling around the world.

Peoples of the North

Materials: copies of the Polar Region Map (page 77); globe, atlas, or world map

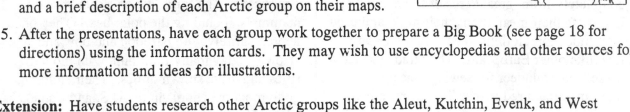

Directions

1. Give a Polar Region map to each student.

2. Divide the class into groups of six. Give each group member an information card about one Arctic people. (See cards below and on next page.)

3. Have each student use a globe, atlas, or world map and the information card to prepare a brief presentation to the small group.

4. During the presentations, have students write in the location and a brief description of each Arctic group on their maps.

5. After the presentations, have each group work together to prepare a Big Book (see page 18 for directions) using the information cards. They may wish to use encyclopedias and other sources for more information and ideas for illustrations.

Extension: Have students research other Arctic groups like the Aleut, Kutchin, Evenk, and West Greenlanders and add them to the Big Book.

The Yakut

The Yakuts live in Siberia in the U.S.S.R. They are the most populous of Asia's Arctic people. They breed both reindeer and dogs for a living. Some Yakuts are so isolated that visitors must use a helicopter to find them. Others work in factories that have recently been built in the far north.

The Nenets

These people are also known as the Samoyeds. They live the farthest north of any Asiatic Arctic people. They herd reindeer and hunt whales and seals for their food. They live in huts dug in the ground. Like most Arctic people, they make large, round drums from the skins of animals.

Peoples of the North *(cont.)*

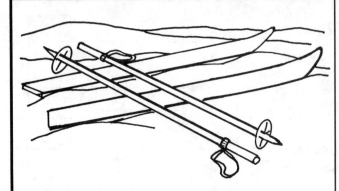

The Lapps of Norway

The Lapps live in northern Europe in the Scandinavian countries of Norway, Sweden and Finland. Their daily necessities once came completely from great herds of reindeer. The Lapps ate their meat, drank their milk, and used their hides for clothing. Today many Lapps live like other Europeans. They trade products made from reindeer for sewing machines and other manufactured items. The Lapps are also credited with inventing snow skis.

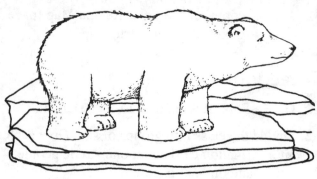

The Inuit Eskimo

These dwellers at the top of North America originally came from Asia like other Native Americans. The Inuit live on a diet of sea mammals, including the polar bear. They once hunted entirely with harpoon and bow and arrow. Today many Inuit hunt with modern rifles and drive snowmobiles. Their children go to modern schools in the U.S. and Canada. About 50,000 Inuits now live in Alaska.

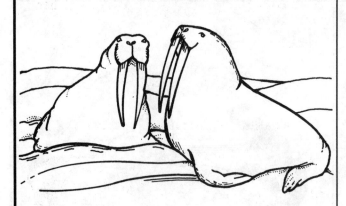

The Polar Eskimo

The Polar Eskimos are the smallest group of people living the farthest north, with some living within 900 miles of the North Pole on the west coast of Greenland. Many Polar Eskimos are completely cut off from other people. They fashion their tools from the bones of sea mammals because they do not have wood or other materials to use.

The Chuckchi

These Asian people live across the Bering Strait in the northeastern corner of the Soviet Union. The Chuckchi live only part of the year above the tree line, retreating in the winter southward into central Siberia. The Chuckchi are believed to be among the first people to live in the Arctic area.

Story Ladder

Write the incidents from *Song of Sedna* in correct order on the lines below.

1. _____
2. _____
3. _____
4. _____
5. _____
6. _____
7. _____
8. _____
9. _____
10. _____
11. _____

Sedna takes a ride on a whale.

Noato throws Sedna into the sea.

Sedna sees Mattak change into a bird.

Sedna becomes goddess of the sea.

Sedna won't marry men who want to marry her.

Seal spirits talk to Sedna.

Sedna shows Mattak how to build an igloo.

Sedna brings Noato and Setka to live with her.

Mattak pursues Noato and Sedna.

Noato comes to rescue Sedna.

Sedna meets Mattak and goes with him.

Readers' Theater

Readers' Theater is a style of performance done by players standing before an audience, using only their voices to create characters and action. In order to perform Readers' Theater, students should understand its unique vocabulary. Review the list below with your students. Use these words when giving rehearsal directions.

Vocabulary

Script—play or story to be read

Rehearsal—practicing the play

Cast—people in the play

Player—what a person who is in the play is called

Understudy—an actor who learns the part of another actor in case he/she is needed to substitute

Upstage—toward the rear of the stage

Downstage—toward the front of the stage

Performance—the actual presentation of the play

Dress Rehearsal—play rehearsal in costume (costumes are optional); last rehearsal before the performance

Bow—bending at the waist to thank audience for their applause

Audience—people who watch the play

Offstage—any area that is not the stage

Applause/Clapping—gesture of gratitude from the audience

Rehearsal

Copy the Readers' Theater script (pages 31-33). Rehearse it several times to give hesitant readers self-confidence. Practice the script with the class using the following suggestions:

1. Model reading—only teacher reads.

2. Echo reading—teacher reads a line and students repeat it.

3. Choral reading—teacher and class read together.

4. Divide the class into five groups, assign each group one of the numbered parts, and read the script using choral speaking. *Select one student who reads well to anchor the group.*

5. Divide the class in pairs and have them quietly read the script to one another by alternating lines.

6. Have five students read the script in front of the class.

Performance

Have five students or five groups perform Readers' Theater in front of the class. Readers' Theater can also be performed with Shadow Puppets (page 34). Ask the class to give complements and offer constructive ideas for improvement. Then perform the play for another class. Readers' Theater is also an excellent idea for Parent Night or other school functions.

Readers' Theater *(cont.)*

(Based on the book Song of Sedna *by Robert D. Sans Souci)*

Part I

1: A long time ago there was a young Eskimo woman named Sedna. She lived near the cold Arctic Ocean with her father Noato, a hunter. Noato's wife had died giving birth to Sedna.

2: Sedna was beautiful and clever, and men came from far away to ask her to marry them. But she found none of them attractive and refused to marry.

3: "You must choose a husband," her father said, "before all of the young men give up and you are left to grow old alone."

4: Sedna answered, "I have seen a man in my dreams. When he comes I will marry him."

5: So things went on like this for awhile. Sedna walked along the shore with her husky named Setka,

1: and many young men returned to their homes sad and unmarried.

2: But one day a mysterious stranger arrived.

3: He was dressed in fancy furs and carried a whalebone harpoon.

4: The prow of his umiak, shaped like the head of a serpent, was strange and terrrifying. "My name is Mattak," he said. "I have come to make you my bride."

5: Surely he was the man in her dreams, but Sedna hesitated,

1: because Setka ran from him,

2: and clouds quickly raced across the sky,

3: and a chilling wind whispered a warning in her ear.

4: But even though her father was not there to give her his advice and though her dog would not follow her into his umiak, she went with him.

5: The two sailed for many days past empty lands, until they came to a small harbor guarded by two gigantic polar bears.

1: They landed in a place where flocks of birds flew overhead and darkened the sun with their wings.

2: Sedna was shocked to find his home nothing but a cave littered with stones and the bones of animals.

Readers' Theater (cont.)

3: In the way of her people, Sedna made an igloo from heavy blocks of ice. She packed the cracks with snow and dug a hole in the top to let the air escape.

4: True to his promises, Mattak gave Sedna meat and the richest and warmest animal furs Sedna had ever seen.

5: One day Mattak went out to hunt, but left his lucky amulet behind, a piece of ivory carved like a raven's foot.

1: Sedna hurried after him. When she saw him, she saw something that filled her with confusion and fear.

2: As she watched him, he changed shape. Growing huge wings, he soared into the sky.

3: Then Sedna realized that she had not married a man, but a demon who could sometimes take on the shape of a man. What could she do?

Part II

4: Meanwhile, Sedna's father, Noato, was worried about his daughter. After asking the shaman to put a protective blessing on his umiak, he set out after her, and found her on the shore of Mattak's island.

5: When Sedna told her father her husband's secret, Noato persuaded his daughter to leave in his umiak without a moment's delay, and off they went, fearfully looking behind them to see if Mattak was pursuing them.

1: When Mattak discovered that Sedna had run away, the heavens shook with the force of his weeping and his angry curses. His demon strength enabled him to change his umiak into a real sea serpent with fire blasting from its jaws.

2: He got closer and closer to Noato and Sedna,

3: but the shaman's blessing kept him from getting too close.

4: Then Mattak gave a loud cry of rage,

5: and spreading his huge wings he flew above Noato's umiak.

1: The water around the boat rose up and cried out, "Send Sedna to us!"

2: and as Mattak dropped closer and closer to the boat, Noato lost his courage.

3: He picked up Sedna and threw her into the sea, thinking that the sacrifice would calm the waters and keep Mattak away.

Readers' Theater *(cont.)*

4: Three times Sedna swam back to the boat, begging her father to help her, but he refused.

5: Finally, exhausted, Sedna sank to the bottom of the sea.

1: Because a blessing was on her, Sedna could walk along the bottom of the sea and breathe like she was on land.

2: As she walked, two banded seals swam by and whispered to her, "Go to the mountain and you will know your destiny."

3: Sedna guessed they were really seal-spirits, so she did as they told her. As she walked ghostly figures swam close to her, telling her to quit, but the two seal-spirits swam by her side and told her to ignore the voices.

4: Just then a ferocious killer whale swam up to her, and Sedna thought she would be killed,

5: but the seal-spirits told her to climb on the whale's back.

1: As she climbed on, the whale turned and looked at her with eyes as cold as ice chips, but it did not attack her.

2: It took her to a huge underwater chasm, over which there was an ice bridge as slender as a knifeblade.

3: "The last task is to cross the bridge on foot," the seal-spirits said.

4: Carefully, Sedna balanced herself and walked across the bridge. On the far side, she found a throne, and when she sat on it, all the creatures of the sea came to her and promised to obey her.

5: The seal spirits said to her, "Now anything you want is in your power, but a kind god uses power with mercy."

1: And that is what Sedna did. She forgave her father and made a home for him under the sea. Sedna lives as sea goddess to this day,

2: and the Eskimos seek her protection whenever they are in danger on the open sea, or when they need food from the ocean to feed their families.

3: Some even say that when the wind blows in a certain way you can hear Sedna singing in her home in the sea.

Shadow Play

Use this activity in conjunction with the Readers' Theater (pages 30-33) or as a separate cooperative learning activity for the whole class.

Materials: slide film projector or other strong light source; copies of silhouettes (pages 34-37); large sheet of white paper; craft sticks or straws; paper and scissors; tape or glue

Directions

1. Explain how a Shadow Play uses silhouettes to represent objects and characters of a story. After reading the story, write two topics, *characters* and *objects*, on the board. Have students name the objects and characters from the story. Discuss how the silhouettes should be drawn to distinguish the different characters. Ask students which character(s) need to have more than one silhouette. (Mattak does because he changes shape.)

2. Have one group of students make shadow puppets while another group practices Readers' Theater. The puppets can be made in several ways. Have each student create two of their own silhouettes in class or for homework, or have students cut out the silhouette shapes from pages 34, 35, and 36. Help students glue or tape the shapes to the ends of craft sticks or straws.

3. Make a shadow theater by suspending a sheet of white paper on a clothesline above a table. Shine a strong light on the paper from behind. Have students kneel behind the table to make their puppets "walk" along the table top. The audience will see the shadows of the puppets appear on the "screen."

4. Have students perform the Shadow Play together with the Readers' Theater.

Extension: Have students create shadow plays for other books they read in class.

Shadow Play *(cont.)*

Shadow Play *(cont.)*

36

Shadow Play *(cont.)*

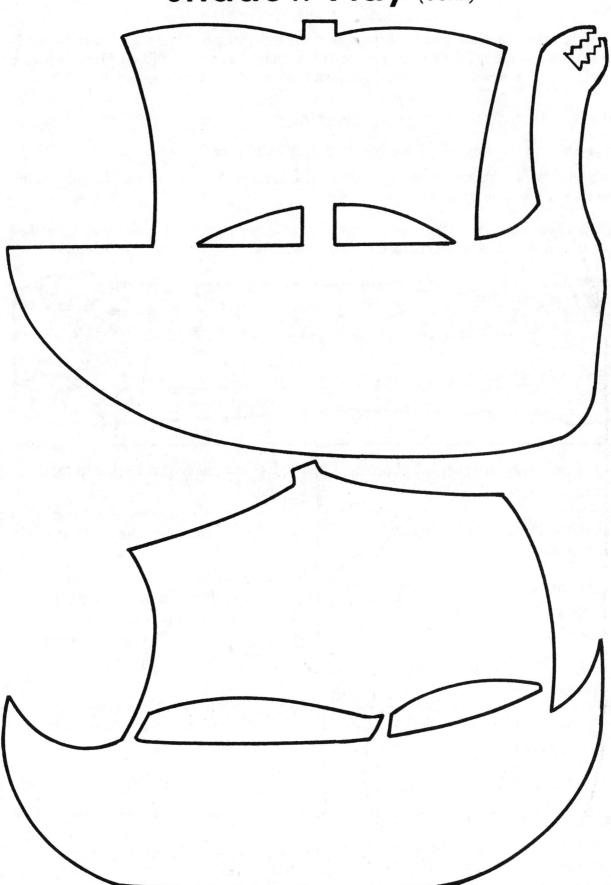

Eskimos: Then and Now

The life of the traditional Eskimo has undergone great change in the past fifty years. It is important for students to overcome the belief that every Eskimo lives in an igloo and hunts with a knife and a harpoon for survival. It is true, however, that some things about Eskimo life have not changed.

Directions

1. Write these categories on a sheet of paper: *Past, Present, Past and Present*.

2. Cut out the fourteen statements about Eskimo Life. Using an encyclopedia to find the information, glue the statements under the correct category.

Extension: Have students write the statements in a Venn diagram. Label one circle: *Past*. Label the second circle *Present*. Label the intersecting parts of the circles: *Past and Present*.

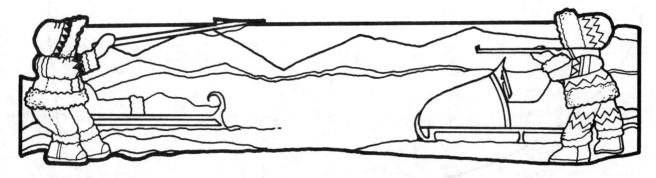

1. The only way to travel is by foot or dogsled.	8. Eskimos have great pride in their tradition.
2. Eskimo hunters use spears and harpoons to hunt.	9. Eskimos eat store-bought food.
3. Eskimos do not know about the way people live in other parts of the world.	10. Eskimo children go to school like other children in their countries.
4. Eskimos use kayaks and umiaks to travel on water.	11. Many Eskimos travel by snowmobile and live in wooden houses.
5. Eskimos hunt seals and whales and catch fish.	12. The Eskimos know a great deal about how to survive in the cold climate.
6. Eskimos follow rules of conduct rather than laws.	13. Some young Eskimos go to college.
7. Eskimos live their entire lives within one cultural group.	14. Eskimos produce beautiful carvings and other items made by hand.

Daily Writing Topics

Mufaro's Beautiful Daughters

1. Write a paragraph describing two kinds of animals that live in Africa.

2. Think of a story that has one good character and one evil character. Contrast the characters in two descriptive paragraphs.

3. Write your own story with good and evil characters.

4. Nyasha is a kind person. Write about a person you think is kind. Give three examples of his or her kindness.

5. Do you think that the king treated Manyara fairly when he showed himself to her as a monster? Why or why not?

6. Do you think Manyara learned a lesson by what happened to her? Why or why not?

7. Write about five things you can do to be kind to others.

8. Write a news report describing the destruction of the African rain forests.

9. Write a story in which you travel down the Nile river. Describe the things you see.

10. Write a report about three kinds of snakes that live in Africa.

Song of Sedna

1. The character, Sedna, has a dog that is very loyal to her. If you could choose a pet, what kind of pet would it be? Describe how you would want this pet to love you. If you already have a pet, describe how it loves you.

2. Sedna lives in the far north. What do you think would be hard about living in a place like the one where she lives?

3. Write a report about polar bears.

4. Write a story about three different animals that live in the Arctic region.

5. Write a paragraph explaining how to build an igloo.

6. If you could breathe underwater like Sedna, what would you do?

7. Think of the times in the story when Sedna needed to be brave. Describe when and why you think Sedna needed to be the bravest.

8. Write about a time in your life when you needed to be brave.

9. Sedna forgave her father even though he was mean to her. Write about someone who has been mean to you. Can you forgive him or her?

Making a Sociogram

A sociogram is a way to analyze the relationships between story characters. This technique can be used for any story with three to five significant characters.

Directions

1. Give students copies of the sociogram on page 41.

2. Have students write the names of characters in the circles and write descriptive sentences about how they think the characters feel about one another on the arrow lines. (See example below.)

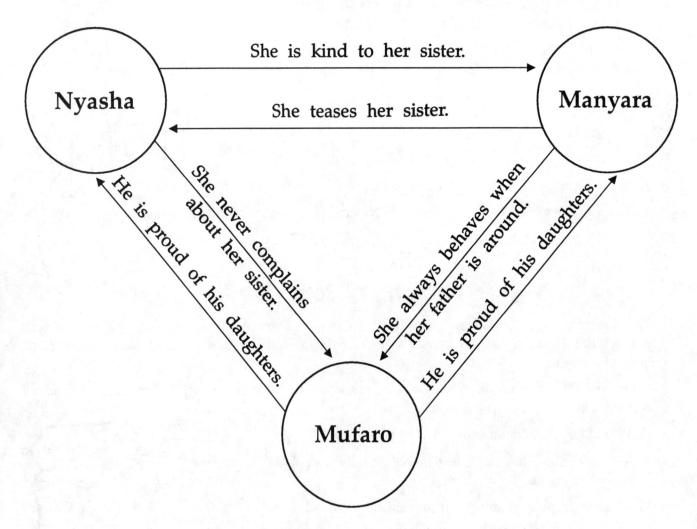

Extensions:

- Do not put names in the circles. Write sentences on the arrow lines and have students identify which character each circle represents by reading the sentences.

- Have students make sociograms about themselves and their friends.

- Have students make sociograms about their families.

Making a Sociogram *(cont.)*

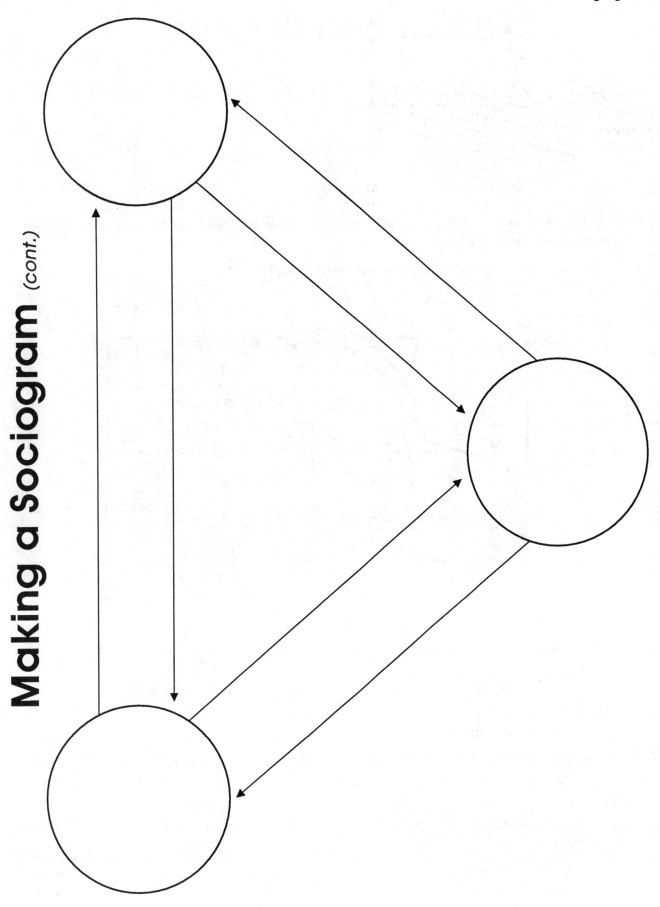

41

Quartering the Story

This technique is a way to focus on four specific aspects of a story. This exercise may be done with both stories in the unit.

Materials: copies of page 43; dictionaries; colored markers or crayons

Directions

1. Reread the story to your students. Explain each of the four sections on page 43 and have students begin working on the questions.

2. Have students use dictionaries to answer the vocabulary question.

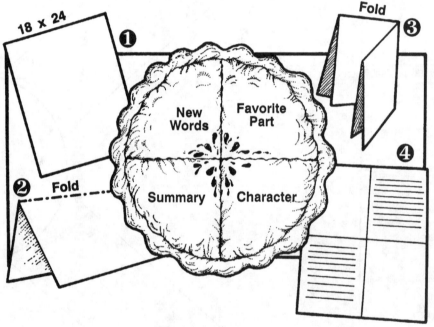

Extension

Use four other questions or ideas to quarter the story. (See examples below.)

Ideas

- Have students make a sociogram in a section. (See Sociogram, page 40.)

- Have students graph two characters in a section. (See Graphing the Characters, page 72.)

- Have students illustrate a scene from the story in a section.

- Have students draw a detailed picture of a character in a section.

Questions

- What is the setting of the story?

- What is the most exciting part of the story?

- What is the conflict or problem in the story? How is it solved?

- Would you have acted the same way as your favorite character from the story? Why or why not?

Quartering the Story (cont.)

A good story needs interesting words. List four new words you found in the story and use a dictionary to find their definitions.

1. _____

_____

2. _____

_____

3. _____

_____

4. _____

_____

Pick one character and write five sentences to describe him or her.

_____
Character

1. _____

2. _____

3. _____

4. _____

5. _____

Draw a picture of your favorite part of the story and write a sentence describing it.

Write a paragraph summarizing the story.

_____

_____

_____

_____

Borrowed Words

A language changes and enriches its vocabulary by borrowing words from other languages and incorporating them into its own. American English has developed from the languages of many ethnic groups. Use a dictionary to write the definition of each African and Eskimo word. Then write the correct word under each picture. **Extension:** Find and illustrate other borrowed words.

African Words	**Eskimo Words**
banjo: _____	kayak: _____
_____	_____
okra: _____	mukluk: _____
_____	_____
banana: _____	igloo: _____
_____	_____
gumbo: _____	parka: _____
_____	_____
tote bag: _____	husky: _____
_____	_____
marimba: _____	umiak: _____
_____	_____

Graphing the Languages

Here are seven of the many languages spoken in Africa, followed by the number (in millions) of people who speak each language. Use the figures and the grid below to make a bar graph to show how many people speak each language.

LANGUAGE	NUMBER OF SPEAKERS (MILLIONS)
Lingala	6
Thonga	3
Feula	12
Shona	7
Tswana	3
Malagasy	11
Ibo	15

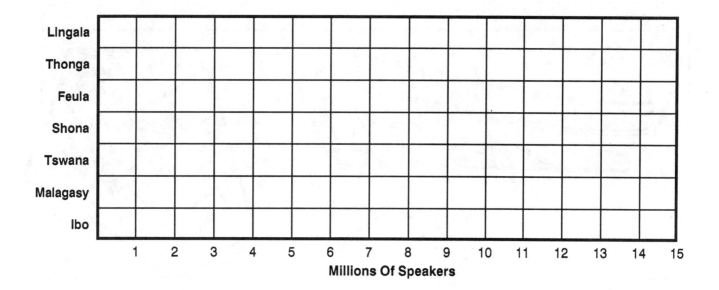

1. What two languages are spoken by the most speakers?

   a. _____ b. _____

2. How many more people speak Feula than Tswana? _____ million people

3. What language is spoken by 12 million speakers? _____

4. How many people speak Malagasy, Shona, and Lingala? _____ million people

5. What two languages are spoken by the fewest speakers?

   a. _____ b. _____

6. How many more people speak Ibo than Lingala? _____ million

Nyasha's Problem

Nyasha is taking her boat across the river. She wants to take a jackal, a bag of millet, and a rooster across with her, but her boat is so tiny she can only take one thing across at a time. What makes it even harder is that Nyasha can't leave the rooster alone on the shore with the jackal because he will eat the rooster. Nyasha can't leave the rooster alone with the millet on the shore either because he will peck a hole in the bag and eat it.

Can you tell Nyasha how she can get the jackal, rooster, and bag of millet across the river safely? Draw a river on a sheet of paper. Then cut out the pictures below. Move them back and forth across the river to find the correct steps to solve Nyasha's problem. Then write the steps in the spaces below.

1. _____

2. _____

3. _____

4. _____

46   © 1992 Teacher Created Materials, Inc.

Counting in Aleut

The Aleut people are related to the Eskimo people both racially and through their language. They live along the south and west coasts of Alaska. Aleut means "brother of the sea otter." They were once a numerous people but today there are only about 8,000 Aleuts left in Alaska.

Use your knowledge of math to find the Aleut words below for the numbers one through ten. Write the Aleut word beside the number at the bottom of the page. Look in the parentheses after the word to find out how to pronounce the number in Aleut.

Clues

- *CANG* (chang) is an odd number between 3 and 7.

- 2 x *CANG* = *ATIQ* (at eek)

- $36 \div 12 = QANKUDIDIM$ (kan koo dee deem)

- 14 - 5 = *SICING* (see ching)

- *ATUNG* (at oong) x *ATUNG* = 36

- *ALAK* (ah lock) + *ALAK* = 4

- 13 - 9 = *SICIN* (see cheen)

- $56 \div 8 = ULLUNG$ (ool loong)

- $72 \div 9 = QAMCING$ (kam sing)

- *AGACA* (ah gaw cha) + 9 = *ATIQ*

1 = _____   6 = _____

2 = _____   7 = _____

3 = _____   8 = _____

4 = _____   9 = _____

5 = _____   10 = _____

Write two of your own math problems here using Aleut numbers.

a. _____

b. _____

Count out loud with a friend from one to ten in Aleut.

Animal Number Clues

Use the clues below to find out about Arctic and African animals.

1. How many teeth does the average killer whale have?

The number is less than 80.

The number is more than 60.

The number is a multiple of 8.

Both digits in the number are even.

_____ teeth

2. In the *Song of Sedna*, Sedna enters a harbor guarded by two, giant polar bears. How many pounds does a polar bear weigh?

The number is a multiple of 100.

The digit in the thousands place is odd.

The number has three zero's.

The number is less than 3000.

_____ pounds

3. How many miles per hour can the average cheetah run?

The number is a multiple of 5.

The number is less than 75.

The number is even.

The number is a multiple of seven.

_____ miles per hour

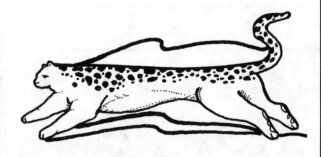

4. In *Mufaro's Beautiful Daughters*, the king takes the shape of a green garden snake. Another green snake that lives in Africa is called the boomslang. How many inches long is the boomslang?

The number is a multiple of 6.

The number is a multiple of 9.

The number is more than 65.

The number is less than 90.

_____ inches

Fresh Water, Salt Water

The ocean is an important resource for providing food and clothing for the people who live in the Arctic. How can this be so if water freezes in cold Arctic temperatures? Compare the freezing process of fresh and salt water using the following experiment.

Materials: school freezer; two identical square cake pans; two science thermometers; measuring cups; identical or very similar objects (such as rocks) to prop up thermometers; salt; water; copies of page 50

Directions

1. Without showing your students, fill one pan with fresh water and the second pan with an equal amount of salt water. (To make salt water, mix 2 tsp/10mg of salt with 2 cups/480mL of water.) Label them **Pan 1** and **Pan 2**.

2. Show the full pans to your students and ask them if they see any differences.

3. Prop a thermometer in a corner of each pan and put them into the school freezer. Have students check the temperatures of the two trays every half hour and make bar graphs of their observations using page 50.

4. After several hours remove the trays and discuss observations and graphs. Ask students to explain how the pans differ. Then ask one student to taste the water from the pan that is not frozen. Explain that salt lowers the freezing temperature of water. Salt water freezes at a colder temperature than fresh water.

5. Ask your students what would happen if the ocean completely froze in the Arctic region. Could people still live there? Why or why not?

Fresh Water, Salt Water *(cont.)*

Use with page 49. Graph the temperatures of the two pans on the graphs below. Use different colors for bars next to each other.

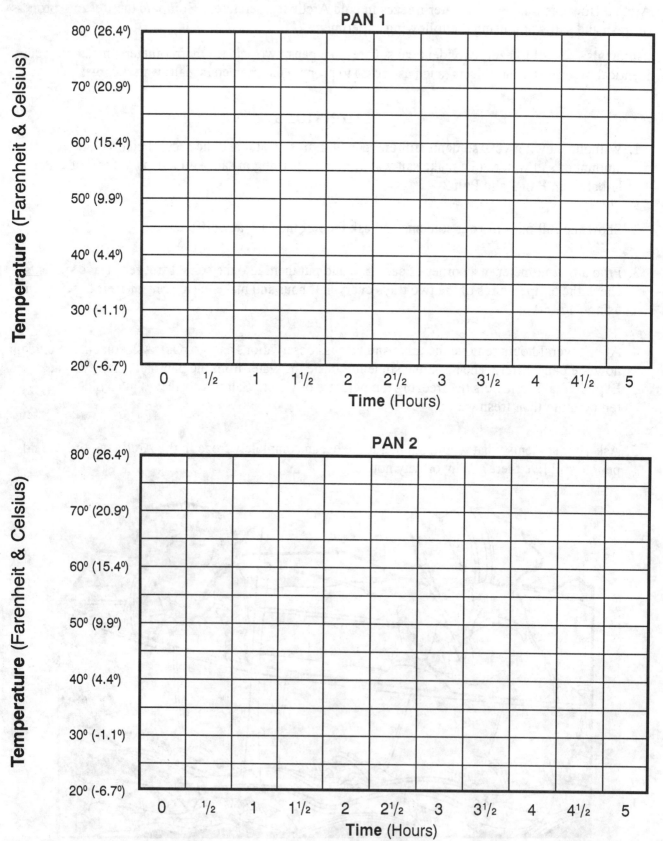

Arctic and African Murals

This cooperative mural activity can be worked on throughout the folk tales unit.

Materials: butcher paper; markers, paints, crayons; scissors; tape; glue; books on Arctic and African animals; encyclopedias; copies of Separating the Animals (page 52), Cape Hunting Dog (page 53), and Animal Research Cards (page 54)

Directions

1. Divide the class into two teams: the Arctic team and the African team. Explain that one team will create an Arctic scene and the other team will create an African scene. Have students select a mural title from the lists below or make up their own. Note that the African team will have to choose a specific area of Africa.

    Africa: Sahara Desert, African Jungle, Nile River, Mount Kilimanjaro, Plains of Africa

    Arctic: Land of the Eskimo, North Pole, Frozen North, Cold Arctic

2. Have students do Separating the Animals (page 52) to help them learn about the animals of each region. Discuss the different challenges animals overcome in order to survive.

3. Have students research the plants, animals, and weather of each region before they start their murals. Do the Cape Hunting Dog activity (page 53) to help students learn how to collect important information. Have students write their research data on Animal Research Cards (page 54).

4. Have each team draw its scenery in pencil on the butcher paper before coloring. Encourage them to include accurate vegetation.

5. Have students draw, cut out, and tape or glue appropriate animals to their murals. They may use the Separating the Animals cards for ideas. Have students label plants, animals, and any important rivers and mountains.

6. Display completed murals.

Separating the Animals

Some of these animals live in the Arctic and some live in Africa. Fold a piece of paper in half. Title one half African Animals and the other Arctic Animals. Cut out the pictures below and glue them to the correct half. Use an encyclopedia or animal book to help you.

kudu

seal

elephant

polar bear

crowned crane

python

snowy owl

wolf

hippopotamus

rhinoceros

serval

reindeer

killer whale

cape hunting dog

gyrfalcon

Cape Hunting Dog

Read the paragraphs below about the cape hunting dog. Fill in the Animal Research Card at the bottom of the page with information from the paragraphs.

When people think of the great predators of Africa, they probably first think of the lion or the leopard. They might be surprised to know that even leopards scramble into trees when a pack of cape hunting dogs comes by. These packs are the most highly organized and efficient hunting teams in Africa. They make their homes in the savannahs of southern and eastern Africa, and they live in groups that range in size from a single family to sixty or more adult members.

A cape hunting dog is short and compact, weighing about forty pounds and measuring four feet in length from its nose to the tip of the its bushy tail. Its fur ranges in color from a mix of yellow, white, and black to pure black or yellow.

Cape hunting dogs feed on the herbivores of the plains, like the reedbuck, impala, Thomson's gazelle, and wildebeest. (Herbivores are animals that eat only plants and other vegetation.) Capable of running for long distances, cape hunting dogs relentlessly chase their prey. Often they drive the prey to where other members of their pack lie in wait. Once the animal is devoured, another hunt begins.

Animal Research Card

Name: _____ Height: _____ Weight: _____

Physical Description: _____

Habitat (Where it lives): _____

Family Life: _____

_____

Special behaviors: _____

_____

Animal Research Cards

Animal Research Card

Name: _____ Height: _____ Weight: _____

Physical Description: _____

Habitat (Where it lives): _____

Family Life: _____

_____

Special behaviors: _____

_____

Animal Research Card

Name: _____ Height: _____ Weight: _____

Physical Description: _____

Habitat (Where it lives): _____

Family Life: _____

_____

Special behaviors: _____

_____

Animal Research Card

Name: _____ Height: _____ Weight: _____

Physical Description: _____

Habitat (Where it lives): _____

Family Life: _____

_____

Special behaviors: _____

_____

Countries of Africa

Materials: copies of pages 56, 57; map of Africa (page 78); encyclopedias and other reference books; glue; scissors; markers; crayons

Directions

1. Make one set of country cards by cutting out the six cards and the six flags from pages 56 and 57. Glue them back to back.

2. Divide the class into six groups. Distribute one country card to each group and a map of Africa to each student. Give each group time to read the information on their card and research further information about the country. Have each student color the country on the map of Africa, write a paragraph about it, and draw pictures of its flag and main products.

3. Regroup the class so that students with the same countries are in different groups. Have students take turns presenting their countries to the group. If necessary, let students check the country cards for extra information.

Extensions:

- Have each student make a full set of country cards. Color the flags using an encyclopedia.

- Have students combine their map pages to make a Big Book. Make dividers for each of the countries.

- Take away the country cards and have the different groups compete to see who knows the most about the countries.

- Have students describe each country flag and draw it on the board from memory.

- Repeat activities for other African countries chosen by students.

Countries of Africa *(cont.)*

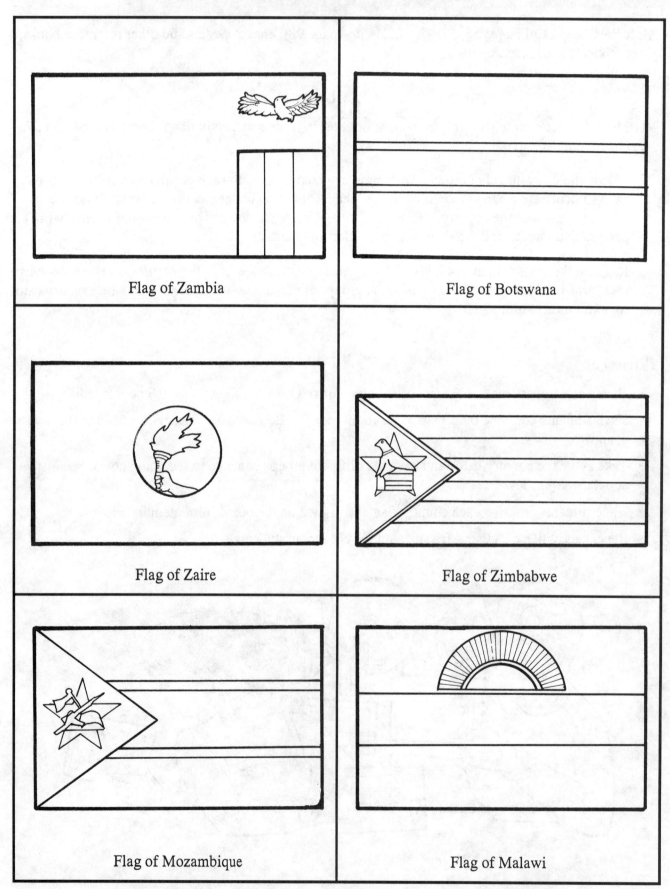

Flag of Zambia

Flag of Botswana

Flag of Zaire

Flag of Zimbabwe

Flag of Mozambique

Flag of Malawi

56

Countries of Africa *(cont.)*

Botswana

Area: about the size of Texas, 231,804 sq. miles (602,690 sq. kilometers)

Capital: Gabarone

Languages: Setswana, English

Main Products: Livestock, corn, peanuts, copper

Money Unit: Pula

Zambia

Area: 290,586 sq. miles (752,614 sq. kilometers)

Capital: Lusaka

Languages: English, Bantu

Main Products: Corn, peanuts, copper cobalt, zinc

Money Unit: Kwacha

Zimbabwe

Area: slightly larger than Montana, 150,803 sq. miles (390,580 sq. kilometers)

Capital: Harare

Languages: Shona, English

Main Products: Chemicals, chromium, cotton

Money Unit: Zimbabwe dollar

Zaire

Area: the size of the United States, 905,000 sq. miles (2,344,885 sq. kilometers)

Capital: Kinshasa

Languages: Bantu, French

Main Products: Copper, coffee, rice, cobalt, sugar cane

Money Unit: Zaire

Malawi

Area: the size of Pennsylvania, 45,747 sq. miles (118,484 sq. kilometers)

Capital: Lilongwe

Languages: Chichewa, English

Main Products: Textiles, tea, rubber, tobacco

Money Unit: Kwacha

Mozambique

Area: the size of Texas, 309,494 sq. miles (799,380 sq. kilometers)

Capital: Maputo

Languages: Bantu, Portuguese

Main Products: Cement, cashews, cotton, coal

Money Unit: Metical

Mapping the Continent

Materials: copies of map on page 78; five crayons of different colors for each student or group.

Directions

1. Explain to students that mapmakers use five colors to ensure that no two countries with common borders have the same color. It is impossible to draw any map for which this isn't true. Five colors will always do the trick.

2. Draw a simple map on the board with only three or four countries. Ask students to imagine they are mapmakers. Ask them how they could color the map so that no adjacent countries have the same color. Could they do it with three colors? Two? Add more countries to the map and have students repeat the activity.

3. Have students try their skills on a real map. Pass out the maps of Africa. Have students brainstorm ways to color the countries before they start coloring so that a mistake does not ruin the map. (Hint: Have students number the countries in pencil before they start coloring.)

4. When students have finished, post the maps and discuss them. Ask students if they see color patterns on their maps.

5. Help students learn the different countries and map skills by asking questions like: Which country is north of Mali?

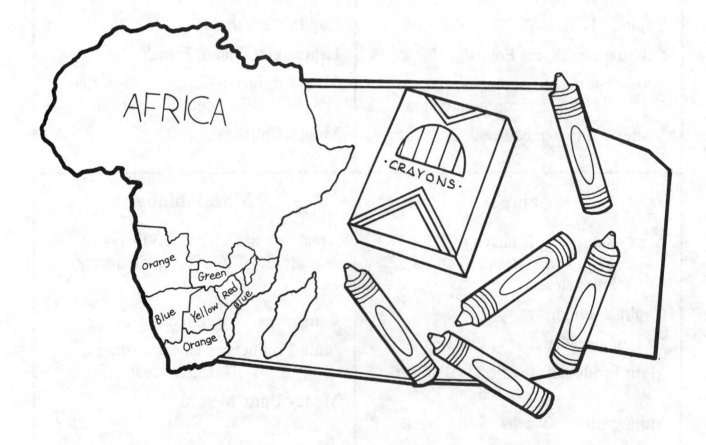

58

Art Projects

How Green Is Your Snake?

Materials: varieties of paper (construction, foil, crepe, cellophane, tissue, etc.) in different shades of green; 18" x 24" (45 x 60 cm) sheets of white construction paper; green markers, pencils, crayons, and paint; scissors; glue

Directions

1. Discuss with your students why green is a good color for a jungle snake. Ask students to think of examples of different shades of green (lime, forest, kelly, avocado, pea, emerald, apple, olive, turquoise, grass, jade, bottle, peacock, dark, yellow-green, etc.)

2. Have students draw outlines of snakes on sheets of construction paper. Challenge students to incorporate many different shades of green into their snake drawings by using the different kinds of paper, green crayons, pencils, and markers.

3. Display the projects in the classroom.

Extension: Have students exchange their snake projects with one another and write stories about them. Encourage students to read their snake stories aloud to the class.

Galimoto

Materials: Copy of *Galimoto* by Karen Lynn Williams if possible (see bibliography); wire of various thicknesses; wire cutters

Directions

1. Ask students to bring in different kinds of wire from home the day before doing this activitiy.

2. Ask your students if they have ever made their own toys. Ask them what kinds of materials they used. Explain that African children make many of their own toys like planes, ships, and cars by twisting wire into various shapes. After the toy is finished, one long wire is attached and used to steer it. Read *Galimoto* to your students if possible.

3. Have students make their own wire toys. Tell students to use thicker wire for the main outline of their toy and thinner wire for other connections. Display the toys. Be sure to give students time to play with their creations.

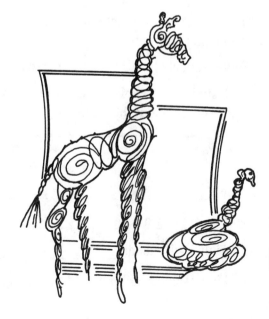

Art Projects *(cont.)*

Sugar Cube Igloos

Materials: sugar cubes; glue; paper plates; cotton balls; 3" x 5" (8 x 13 cm) cards

Directions

1. Have students glue sugar cubes together on paper plate bases to make igloos. They may glue on cotton balls for snow.

2. Have students write a paragraph describing their projects on 3" x 5" (8 x 13 cm) cards. Place them next to their igloos. (Option: Have students give oral presentations about their projects.)

3. Display igloo projects in the classroom.

Making an Amulet

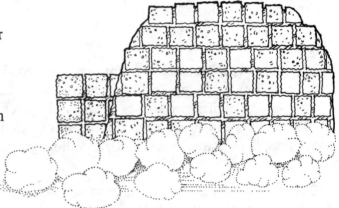

In *Song of Sedna*, Sedna wears a necklace with a picture of a sea animal carved into a piece of stone or leather. Mattak also has a piece of ivory carved like a raven's foot. These objects are called amulets, and they are made by people in many cultures. Amulets supposedly have magic powers to bring good luck and protect people from bad things. Amulets are often made in the shape of animals.

Materials: clay; twigs; small wooden blocks; string; markers; paint

Directions

1. Explain amulets to your students. Find pictures of amulets in the library to show your students.

2. Have students complete the lower half of this page as homework and bring in necessary materials to make their amulets.

3. Give students time in class to make their amulets. Display them in the classroom.

4. Ask students to explain their amulets to the class and what makes them lucky. Have students write a paragraph about their amulets.

My Amulet

Name _____

I will be making a _____

Materials I will need: _____

The kind of good luck I would like my amulet to bring me _____

_____

African Games

Discuss games your students know that involve simple objects like rope, sticks, stones, marbles, etc. Ask students if they have ever made up games of their own. Discuss how children all over the world have played games throughout history. Explain that African children have played the games described below for hundreds of years.

Ohoro

Materials: paper egg cartons; 48 beans, nuts, or pebbles for each pair of players

Directions: The object of the game is to win the most beans. Begin the game by placing four beans in each of the twelve egg carton cups. The first player begins by taking four beans from any cup and placing them, one by one, going clockwise into the next four cups. These cups will now have five beans in them. The same player then takes the beans from the cup into which he/she put the last bean and places these beans, one by one, into the next five cups. The player continues picking up beans and placing them in cups.

A player wins beans by putting the last bean of that move into a cup with three others to make four. The player then takes the beans. However, if a player places a bean into a cup with three others, and the bean is not the last bean of his/her move, then the opponent gets the four beans.

A player's turn ends when he/she puts a bean into an empty cup. Then the other player chooses a cup to start from and begins his/her turn. The last player to win four beans wins the remaining beans on the board. The player with the most beans wins.

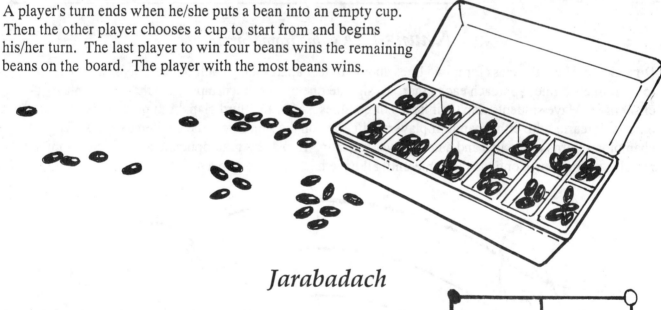

Jarabadach

Materials: three black stones, three white stones, sheet of paper

Directions: The objective is to get three stones in a row like tic-tac-toe. Draw a large square on a sheet of paper and divide it into four equal squares. One player has three black stones and the other has three white ones. Players take turns putting one stone at a time on one of the nine points where the lines of the squares intersect. If neither player has three stones in a row after all stones have been played, players take turns moving their stones to an adjacent, empty point until one player does get three stones in a row.

African Games *(cont.)*

Kuwakha Nchuwa

Materials: A pile of small pebbles or beans

Directions: The object of the game is to win the most pebbles. This is a game for two or more players or teams. A player picks a pebble from the pile and tosses it into the air. With the same hand, the player must pick up a second pebble from the pile and catch the first pebble before it falls to the ground. If the player is successful, he/she places the pebbles in front of him/her and takes another turn. If unsuccessful, the player returns the two pebbles to the pile. Each player gets 10 tries to win as many pebbles as possible. The player or team with the most pebbles after all the players have had their turns wins the game.

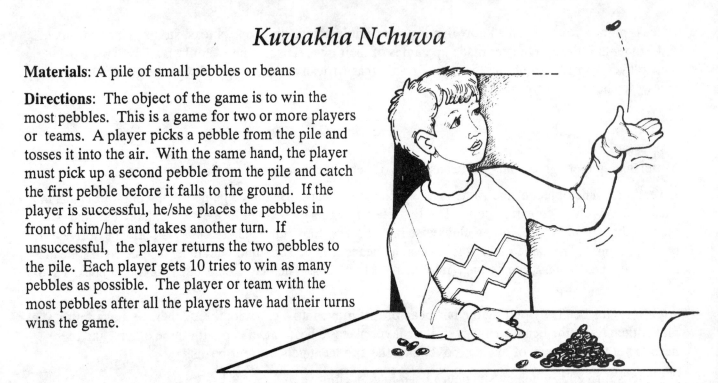

Nnunsa *(A game from Zaire)*

Directions: Have the class form two lines about six feet apart facing each other   Have two students (one from each line) approach each other. Designate one player the champion and the second player the challenger. Have students clap their hands three times. After the third clap, both players try to clasp the other's forearm with either hand. If players join arms on the same side, the challenger wins. The champion returns to the line and a new player steps up. If players grab opposite arms, the champion remains champion. Continue the game until all have had a chance to play.

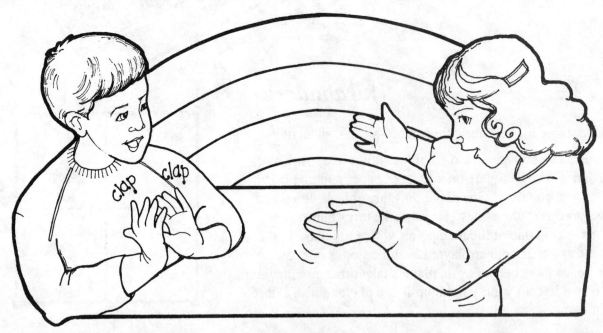

Eskimo Games

Spearing the Bone

Eskimos play this clever game with a piece of bone or ivory and animal sinew.

Materials: 18-inch length of string; pencil or ³/₈" (1 cm) wooden dowel; small round piece of wood with one or more ¹/₂" (1.25 cm) holes drilled in it

Directions: Tie one end of the string to the pencil and the other end to the piece of wood. (See diagram.) The object of the game is to spear the piece of wood with the pencil by swinging the piece of wood upward and trying to insert the pencil or wood "spear" into the hole.

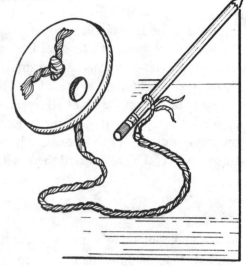

Nuglutang

Materials: four pencils or ³/₈" (1 cm) wooden dowels; string or yarn; wood or cardboard with ¹/₂" (1.25 cm) hole in it; small weight

Directions: Assemble the string, wood, and weight as shown. Suspend the piece of wood from a support. Twirl the weight to set the wood spinning. Two to four players try to insert their pencils into the hole. The first player to do so is the winner.

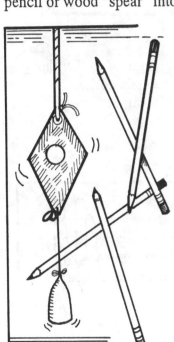

Bones in a Bag

Eskimos play this game with a leather bag, several small carved bones (which can be assembled to represent an igloo scene), and a leather thong tied like a noose.

Materials: string; paper bag; four or five identical sets of small plastic animals, human figures, or other small objects

Directions: Players take turns lowering the string noose into the bag to capture a figurine. Each player only has 15 seconds per turn. The first player to capture enough pieces to complete a set is the winner.

Eskimo Games *(cont.)*

Igdlukitaqtung

Materials: tennis balls or other small balls

Directions: The first challenge is to pronounce the name of this game! This game is a form of Eskimo juggling and is not competitive. The player takes two small balls and throws them from the right hand to the left. The object of the game is to keep one ball in the air at all times and tell a story, sing a song, or recite a poem at the same time. Demonstrate the game to your class. Your students will be more likely to try it themselves if you have amused them with your own attempts.

Cat's Cradle

Eskimos make amazingly intricate representations of people and animals using a length of leather thong or animal sinew tied together at the ends. Eskimos make the representations as they tell stories. For more string ideas see *String Figures and How to Make Them* by Caroline Jayne (Dover, 1906) and *Games of the World* by UNICEF (Plenary Publications Intl., 1975).

Materials: 3-foot (1 m) piece of string

Directions:

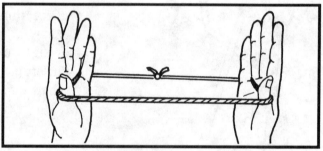

1. Tie the ends of the string together. Start with the string looped around your thumbs and little fingers.

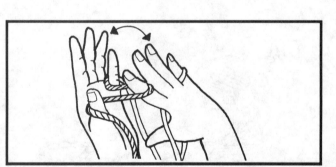

2. Loop your right index finger under the string on your left hand, and the left index finger under the string on your right hand.

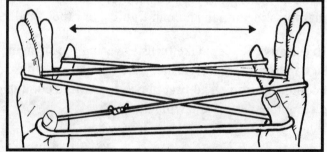

3. Pull both hands apart. The string should look like the picture to the right.

   Make string pictures by looping the string over your hands and use your fingers to intertwine the string. See the references listed above for variations of cat's cradle. Page 65 illustrates one variation.

64

Eskimo Games (cont.)

Fish Spear *(A variation of cat's cradle)*

1. Start with the string looped around your thumbs and little fingers.

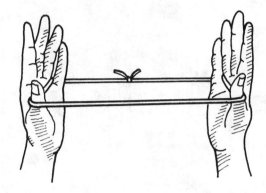

2. Loop your right index finger under the string on your left hand.

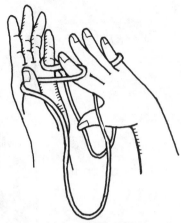

The string should look like this:

3. Twist it down away from you and up toward you twice as you pull your hands apart.

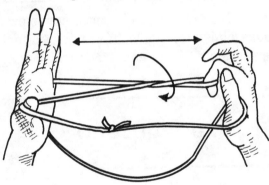

4. Pass your left index finger down through the loop over your right index finger and pick-up the string that crosses your palm from underneath. Pull your hands apart. The string should look like this:

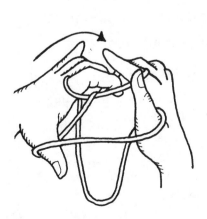

5. Release the loops from around your right thumb and little finger. Pull your right index finger to tighten the figure. The string should look like this:

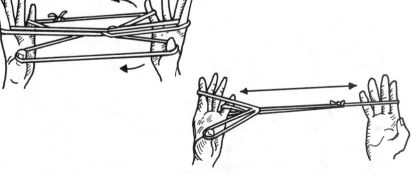

The three loops represent the three prongs of a fishing spear and the long loop is the spear itself.

African Recipes

African Yam Fritters

Ingredients

1½ pounds (.750 kg) of yams

1 egg

1 chopped onion

1 chopped tomato

1 small green chile, minced

½ cup (125 mL) bread crumbs

peanut oil

Pinch of cayenne pepper

Salt and pepper

Boil, peel and mash yams. Beat egg. Sauté tomato, chile, and onion in peanut oil until onion is transparent and soft. Combine sautéed mixture, egg, bread crumbs, seasonings, and yams. Form mixture into patties and brown on both sides. Eat! Makes ten small servings.

Peanut Soup

Ingredients

1 tbs. (15 mL) butter

1 cup (250 mL) chopped onion

2 tsp. (10 mL) fresh ginger root

Salt and pepper to taste

Dash each of cinnamon, and cloves

1 cup (250 mL) chopped raw peanuts

2 cups (500 mL) chicken stock

½ cup (125 mL) raisins

1 tbs. (15 mL) honey

½ cup (125 mL) peanut butter

1½ cups (375 mL) milk or buttermilk

Sauté onion, ginger, salt, and pepper in butter until onions become clear. Add cinnamon, cloves, and peanuts and sauté 5-10 minutes. Stir in chicken stock, raisins, honey, and peanut butter. Mix thoroughly. Cover and simmer over low heat for one hour. Add milk and serve when soup is hot. Makes ten small servings.

66

Folk Tales From Around the World

A Folk Tale Research Center

Objective

The purpose of this center is to help students develop an awareness of different cultures from around the world through detailed study of folk tales. Students can do the worksheets individually or work in groups to create their own folk tales research projects.

Preparation

1. Make your research center according to the diagram on page 69. Remember that your center can be used year after year, so taking time to make a permanent center by coloring and laminating graphics will pay off later.

2. Assemble a collection of folk tales. Have students bring in their own favorites from home or their public library. Give them homework credit as an incentive. Have them bring in magazines and books showing the cultures of different countries.

3. Reproduce pages 70-76, and place them in manila envelopes. Attach the envelopes to your center and write appropriate titles.

4. Enlarge the world map from page 76. Color and attach it to the middle section of the center. Draw or cut out pictures from magazines of objects from different countries and glue them to your center.

5. Allow six to eight 30-45 minute class periods for students to complete the different activities in this project.

Procedure

1. Have students read folk tales for one or two class periods. Then introduce the research center and explain the worksheets. For each folk tale they read, have students complete a Folk Tale Research Sheet (page 71), and What Is a Folk Tale? (page 70). In addition, have students write down unique vocabulary words (page 73). They should complete a folk tale origin slip (page 74) and glue or tape it to their world maps. (Options: Have students attach their folk tale origin slips to the large world map on the research center. Or, have groups of students make and color their own large world maps on large sheets of poster board and attach the origin slips.) Use the map to call on students to give one-minute summaries of the folk tales they have read.

Folk Tales From Around the World
(cont.)

2. After students have had a chance to read several folk tales have them do a Venn diagram (page 75) of two stories and graph important characters (page 72). Demonstrate the Venn diagram and Character Graph for your students. See pages 19 and 20 for an example of a Venn diagram comparing two stories. Use the example below to show how graphs can be used to compare Nyasha and Manyara. For Nyasha, the X was placed in the upper left corner of the graph because she is both good and smart. The X was placed in the lower right corner of the graph for Manyara because she is bad and foolish.

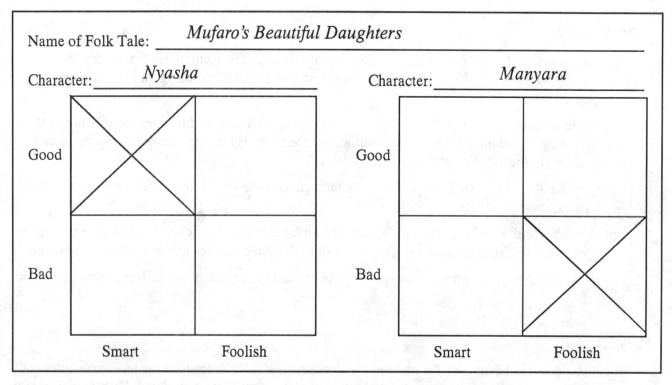

Name of Folk Tale: ___*Mufaro's Beautiful Daughters*___

Character: ___*Nyasha*___   Character: ___*Manyara*___

3. Have groups of students make a folk tales Big Book by organizing their worksheets in a 3-ring binder. Give groups time to discuss book organization, do illustrations for each folk tale, and think of a unique title. Here are some other ideas for groups to research: folk tales from the same country, folk tales about the same topic (wisdom, marriage, origin of something, bravery, etc.), different versions of the same folk tale, comparisons of bad characters, and comparisons of good characters. Make the books available at the research center for other groups to read.

Tips on Managing the Cooperative Group

If you decide to use the research center as a cooperative learning activity, give each member of the group a distinct responsibility. Here are some ideas:

One member keeps the world map up-to-date by attaching origin slips to the correct country.

One member reports to the whole class about what folk tale topic his/her group is researching. (Be sure to schedule a time each day for these reports.)

One member maintains any supplies the group needs.

One member compiles and organizes the folk tale book that the group will present to the class.

Folk Tale Research Center

Vocabulary Sheets

What Is a Folk Tale?

Venn Diagrams

Folk Tales from Around the World

For this project you will:

1. _____
2. _____
3. _____
4. _____
5. _____
6. _____

Graphing the Characters

Research Sheets

Folk Tale Originals

World Maps

To make this center you will need:

3 large sheets of posterboard

1 sheet posterboard for each group

copies of pages 70-76

9" x 12" envelopes to use as holders

collections of folk tales, world atlases, magazines, reference materials

a 3-ring binder for each small group

markers, crayons, colored pencils

masking tape, clear tape

pushpins

yarn

scissors

What Is a Folk Tale?

A folk tale is a story or legend handed down from generation to generation usually by oral retelling. Folk tales often explain something that happens in nature or convey a certain truth about life.

The following elements are often found in most folk tales:

- The beginning of the story starts with "Once upon a time..." or a similar phrase.
- Magic events, characters, and objects are part of the story.
- One character is someone of royalty (king, queen, prince, princess, etc.).
- One character is wicked.

- One character is good.
- Goodness is rewarded in the story.
- Certain numbers like three and seven are in the story (three eggs, seven sisters, etc.).
- The story ends with "... they lived happily ever after."

Identify the elements of each folk tale you read in the spaces below. Write specific examples.

Folk Tale Record Sheet

Name of Folk Tale: _____

Story beginning: _____

Magic: _____

Royalty: _____

Wicked character(s): _____

Good character(s): _____

Goodness rewarded: _____

Numbers in the story (3 or 7): _____

Story ending: _____

Folk Tale Research Sheet

Name of Story: _____

Country of Origin: _____

Main Character(s): _____

Other Important Character(s):

_____

_____

_____

Summary: _____

_____

_____

_____

_____

_____

What test or problem do the main characters face?

_____

_____

_____

_____

_____

How is the problem solved? _____

_____

_____

_____

_____

Graphing the Characters

Mark an X in the appropriate box of each grid below to graph the qualities of the main characters from two folk tales.

Name of Folk Tale: _____

Character: _____   **Character:** _____

	Smart	Foolish
Good		
Bad		

	Smart	Foolish
Good		
Bad		

Name of Folk Tale: _____

Character: _____   **Character:** _____

	Smart	Foolish
Good		
Bad		

	Smart	Foolish
Good		
Bad		

• Use specific examples from the folk tales to write a paragraph about two characters from your graphs who are similar.

• Write a paragraph contrasting the qualities of two characters.

• Think of other character qualities (sad, happy, ugly, beautiful) and make your own graphs for the characters from the folk tales you read.

Folk Tale Vocabulary

One way to compare folk tales is to look at the words writers use. Read three folk tales and list four difficult words from each folk tale on the lines below. Use a dictionary to find the definition of each word. Compare your lists with other students in your class or group. Did you find some of the same words?

Name of Folk Tale: _____

        Word   *Definition*

1. _____ : _____

2. _____ : _____

3. _____ : _____

4. _____ : _____

Name of Folk Tale: _____

        Word   *Definition*

1. _____ : _____

2. _____ : _____

3. _____ : _____

4. _____ : _____

Name of Folk Tale: _____

        Word   *Definition*

1. _____ : _____

2. _____ : _____

3. _____ : _____

4. _____ : _____

Folk Tale Origins

As you read folk tales from around the world, fill out a slip below for each story and attach it to your world map. Connect the slip to the place on the world map where the folk tale originated.

Story Title: _____ _____ _____ Origin: _____ Read By: _____	Story Title: _____ _____ _____ Origin: _____ Read By: _____	Story Title: _____ _____ _____ Origin: _____ Read By: _____
Story Title: _____ _____ _____ Origin: _____ Read By: _____	Story Title: _____ _____ _____ Origin: _____ Read By: _____	Story Title: _____ _____ _____ Origin: _____ Read By: _____
Story Title: _____ _____ _____ Origin: _____ Read By: _____	Story Title: _____ _____ _____ Origin: _____ Read By: _____	Story Title: _____ _____ _____ Origin: _____ Read By: _____
Story Title: _____ _____ _____ Origin: _____ Read By: _____	Story Title: _____ _____ _____ Origin: _____ Read By: _____	Story Title: _____ _____ _____ Origin: _____ Read By: _____
Story Title: _____ _____ _____ Origin: _____ Read By: _____	Story Title: _____ _____ _____ Origin: _____ Read By: _____	Story Title: _____ _____ _____ Origin: _____ Read By: _____

Folk Tale Venn Diagram

Use the pattern below to make Venn diagrams from the folk tales you read. In the intersecting parts of the circle, write the things the two folk tales have in common. In the other parts write the things that make the stories different.

Folk Tale: _____

Folk Tale: _____

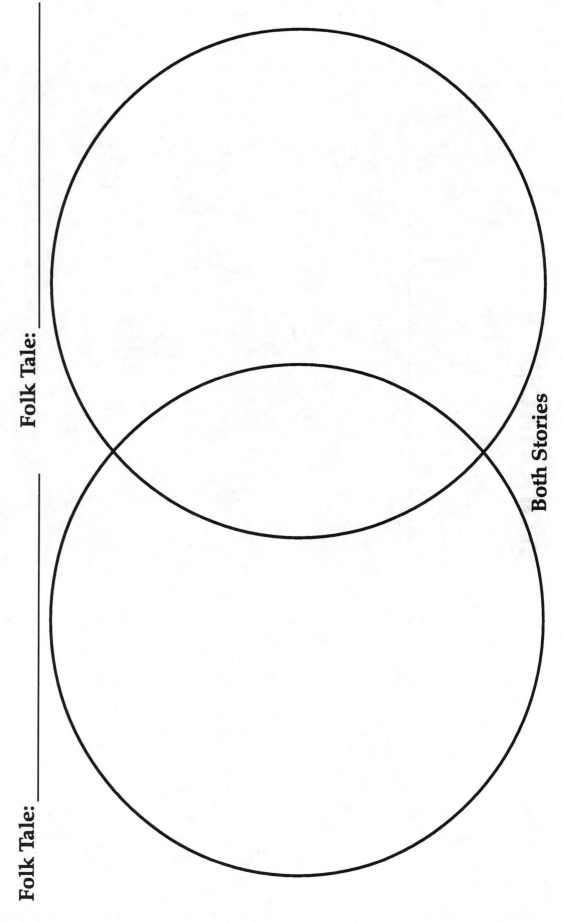

Both Stories

World Map

Polar Region Map

Use with page 27.

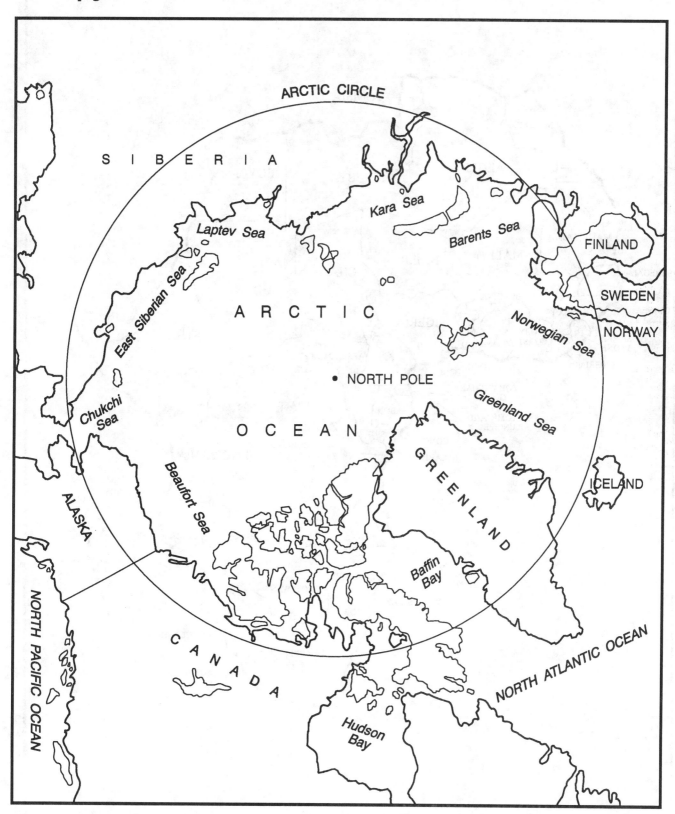

Map of Africa

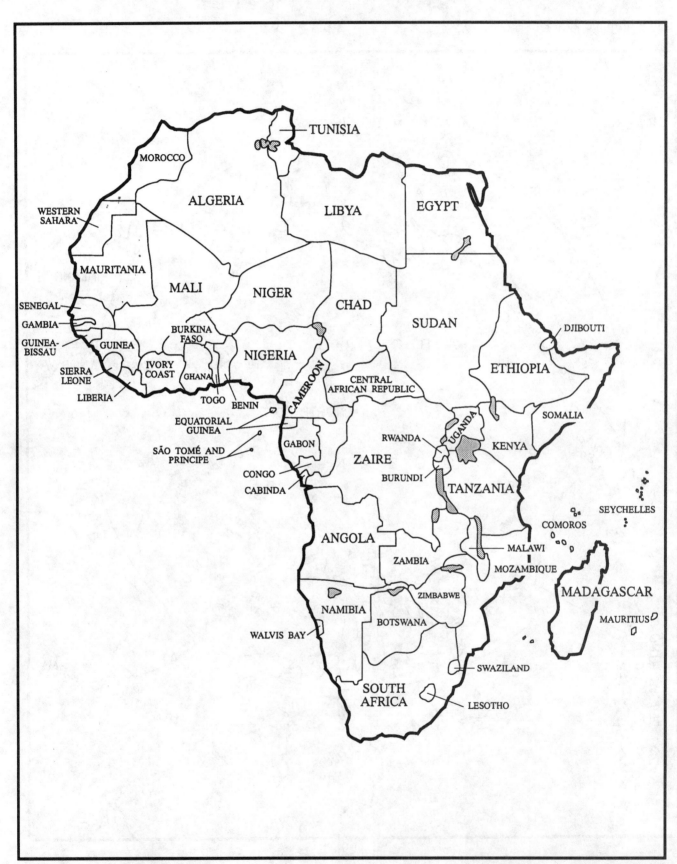

78

Bibliography

Collections of Folk Tales

Berger, Terry. *Black Fairy Tales.* (Atheneum Press, 1969) This collection has another version of Mufaro called *Baboon Skins* and another version of *The Talking Eggs* called *The Three Little Eggs.*

Cole Joanna (selected by). *Best-Loved Folktales of the World.* (Doubleday, 1982)

Crouch, Marcus (ed.). *The Whole World Storybook.* (Oxford, 1983)

Grimm, Brothers (collected by). *The Complete Grimm's Fairy Tales.* (Random House, 1972)

Jagendorf, M.A. (ed.). *Noodlehead Stories From Around the World.* (Vanguard, 1957)

Phelps, E. J. *The Maid of the North: Feminist Folk Tales From Around the World.* (Henry Holt, 1981)

Sierra, Judy and Robert Kaminski. *Multicultural Folktales.* (Onyx Press, 1991)

Thompson, Stith (ed.). *One Hundred Favorite Folktales.* (Indiana U. Press, 1968)

Yolen, Jane (edited by). *Favorite Folktales From Around the World.* (Random House, 1986)

Tales from Africa

Aardema, Verna.
  Bimwili & Zimwi: A Tale from Zanzibar. (Dial, 1985)
  Bringing the Rain to Kapiti Plain: A Nandi Tale. (Dial, 1981)
  Oh Kojo! How Could You! An Ashanti Tale. (Dial, 1984)
  Princess Gorilla and A New Kind of Water. (Dial, 1988)
  Rabbit Makes a Monkey of a Lion. (Swahili) (Dial, 1989)
  Traveling to Tondo: A Tale of the Nkundo of Zaire. (Knopf, 1991)
  The Vinganance and the Tree Toad: A Liberian Tale. (Warne, 1983)

  What's So Funny, Ketu? (Sudanese) (Dial, 1982)
  Who's in Rabbit's House? A Masai Tale. (Dial, 1977)
  Why Mosquitos Buzz in People's Ears: A West African Tale. (Dial, 1975)

Arkhurst, J. C. *The Adventures of Spider: West African Folktales.* (Scholastic, 1964)

Bryan, Ashley. *Beat the Story Drum, Pum Pum.* (Macmillan, 1980)

Greaves, Nick. *When Hippo Was Hairy: And Other Tales From Africa.* (Barron's, 1988)

Hailey, Gail E. *A Story, A Story.* (Macmillan, 1970)

San Souci, Robert D. *The Talking Eggs.* (Dial, 1989) American version of an African tale.

Steptoe, John. *Mufaro's Beautiful Daughters: An African Tale.* Lothrop, (1987)

Tales from the Cold North

Caswell, Helen (ed.). *Shadows from the Singing House: Eskimo Folk Tales.* (Tuttle, 1968)

De Armand, Dale. *Berry Woman's Children.* (Greenwillow, 1985)
  The Seal Oil Lamp. (Sierra, 1988)

de Wit, Dorothy, ed. *The Talking Stone.* (Greenwillow, 1979) Includes another version of Sedna.

Hewitt, Garnet. *Ytek and the Arctic Orchid: An Inuit Legend.* (Vanguard, 1981)

Houston, James. *The Falcon Bow: An Arctic Legend.* (Macmillan, 1986)
  Tikta' liktak: An Eskimo Legend. (Harcourt, 1965)
  The White Arches: An Eskimo Legend. (Harcourt, 1979)

Martin, Eva. *Tales of the Far North.* (Dial, 1986)

Mayer, Mercer. *East of the Sun and West of the Moon.* (Macmillan, 1980)

Melzack, Ronald. *The Day Tuk Became a Hunter and Other Stories.* (Dodd, Mead, and Thompson, 1971) Includes another version of Sedna.

San Souci, Robert D. *Song of Sedna.* (Doubleday, 1981)

Nonfiction
Africa

Laure, Jason. *Zimbabwe.* (Children's Press, 1988)

Lye, Keith. *Africa.* (Gloucester Press, 1987)

Murphy, E. Jefferson. *The Bantu Civilization of Southern Africa.* (Thomas E. Crowell Company, 1974)

Musgrove, Margaret. *Ashanti to Zulu.* (Dial, 1976)

O'Toole, Thomas. *Zimbabwe...in Pictures.* (Lerner Publications, 1988)

Williams, Karen Lynn. *Galimoto.* (Lothrop, 1990)

Eskimo

Bringle, Mary. *Eskimos.* (Franklin Watts, 1973)

Jenness, Aylette and Alice River. *In Two Worlds: A Yup'ik Eskimo Family.* (Houghton Mifflin, 1989)

Petty, Kate. *Eskimos.* (Gloucester Press, 1987) Third grade reading level.

Language

Flexner, Stuart Berg. *I Hear America Talking.* (Simon and Schuster, 1976) A fascinating compendium on the origins of spoken English words.

Answer Key

Page 7

1)*tata*-father 2)*iduba*-flower 3)*syaanza*-lion 4)*sokwe*-monkey 5)*wa buka*-good morning 6)*ingoma*-drum 7)*mwana*-child 8)*musa*-friend 9)*nda lumba*-thank you 10)*bamama*-mother 11)*mwezi*-moon 12)*inzovu*-elephant

Page 10

1)Sahara Desert 2)Atlas Mountains 3)Kalahari Desert 4)Zambezi River 5)Mt. Kilimanjaro 6) Nile River 7)Congo River 8)Aswan Dam 9)Lake Nasser 10)Atlantic Ocean 11)Lake Victoria 12)Red Sea 13)equator 14)veld 15)Mediterranean Sea 16)Mt. Toubkai 17)Indian Ocean 18)tropical rain forests

Page 12

1)Great Zimbabwe was a great city built in 1100 A.D. 2)A great stone wall surrounded the city. 3)Many detailed objects were built in the city 4)The city was deserted between 1500 A.D. and 1800 A.D.

The chevron pattern is on the page where Manyara rushes out of the king's chamber and sees Nyasha.

The soapstone birds are on the page where Nyasha sees Nyoka in the king's chamber.

The conical tower is visible on the same page as the chevron pattern and on the double page spread of the wedding behind the drapes.

Page 17

1)A man.. 2)Manyara was.. 3)The king.. 4)Mufaro.. 5)Manyara met.. 6)Later.. 7)The next.. 8)Nyasha gave.. 9)When.. 10)She had.. 11)But.. 12)Instead.. 13)The two.. 14)Manyara became..

Page 19

Mufaro's Beautiful Daughters: 4,6,9
Makanda Mahlanu: 2,3
Both stories: 1,5,7,8

Page 29

1)Sedna won't.. 2)Sedna meets.. 3)Sedna shows... 4)Sedna sees.. 5)Noato comes.. 6)Mattak.. 7)Noato throws.. 8)Seal.. 9)Sedna takes.. 10)Sedna becomes.. 11)Sedna brings..

Page 38

Past: 1,2,3,4,6,7
Present: 9,10,11,13
Both: 5,8,12,14

Page 44

banjo: four-stringed musical instrument with a body like a tambourine
okra: tall plant with sticky green pods used to thicken soup
banana: curved, yellow fruit
gumbo: chicken and rice soup thickened with okra
tote bag: large handbag
marimba: wooden, musical instrument like a xylophone
kayak: Eskimo canoe made of animal skins stretched over a light frame of wood or bone
mukluk: fur-lined, seal skin boot worn by Eskimos
igloo: Eskimo hut usually built out of ice blocks
parka: fur jacket with a hood worn in cold regions
husky: Eskimo dog used to pull sleds
umiak: large Eskimo boat

Page 45

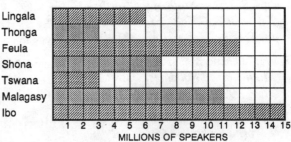

1)a.Ibo b. Feula 2)9 million 3)Feula 4)24 million 5)a.Thonga b.Tswana 6)9 million

Page 46

1)Take rooster across. 2)Take jackal across and bring rooster back. 3)Drop off rooster and take millet across. 4)Return to other side to get rooster and bring him across.

Page 47

1=*agaca*, 2=*alak*, 3=*qankudidim*, 4=*sicin*, 5=*cang*, 6=*atung*, 7=*ullung*, 8=*qamsing*, 9=*sicing*, 10=*atiq*

Page 48

1)64 teeth 2)1000 lbs. 3)70 mph 4)72 in.

Page 52

Africa: kudu, crowned crane, rhinoceros, serval, cape hunting dog, elephant, python, hippopotamus
Arctic: polar bear, snowy owl, killer whale, seal, wolf, reindeer, gyrfalcon